TIME FOR KIDS

Start Exploring

Nonfiction Reading in Social Studies

SHELL EDUCATION

Credits

Editors
Christina Hill, M.A.
Conni Medina

Assistant Editor
Leslie Huber, M.A.

Senior Editor
Lori Kamola, M.A.Ed.

Editor-in-Chief
Sharon Coan, M.S.Ed.

Editorial Manager
Gisela Lee, M.A.

Creative Director
Lee Aucoin

Cover Design
Robin Erickson

Illustration Manager/Designer
Timothy J. Bradley

Interior Layout Design
Robin Erickson

Print Production
Phil Garcia

Publisher
Corinne Burton, M.A.Ed.

Shell Education
5301 Oceanus Drive
Huntington Beach, California 92649
http://www.shelleducation.com

ISBN 978-1-4258-0452-7

Table of Contents

Introduction

How to Use This Product

Start Exploring Nonfiction Reading in Social Studies has been designed to enhance your reading program. The activities will motivate students to want to read with **high-interest**, **nonfiction content** and **engaging photographs**. Moreover, the authentic nonfiction reading experiences these activities provide can help students develop **vocabulary**, **comprehension**, and **fluency** skills in accordance with Reading First legislation. Within each unit of study, you will find easy-to-follow lesson plans and reading comprehension strategies ideal for your Pre-K, kindergarten, and first grade students. Each lesson is correlated to both Pre-K and K–2 standards. For more information, see Correlation to Standards (pages 19–21).

Each unit includes a set of activity cards based on a theme. The four themes in this book are **My Community**, **Community Workers**, **Kinds of Land and Water**, and **The United States**. Each card includes activities for **activating prior knowledge**, **skills for language development**, and new ideas for **building knowledge and comprehension**. These activities are especially important for ELL and below-level students. The activity cards can be taught separately or in conjunction with the lessons. The lessons provide ideas for teaching the cards in a variety of ways, including whole-class lessons and small-group centers.

Each unit contains **two introductory lessons** that teach specific reading comprehension skills, followed by **focus lessons** and **centers** to **reinforce students' comprehension**. The **wrap-up lesson** found at the end of each unit combines and reinforces the skills taught throughout the unit. The **student reproducible pages** (found at the end of each unit) are used for practice and comprehension. These pages are usually distributed during one of the center activities. Also, consider using the activity sheets as assessments for reading comprehension.

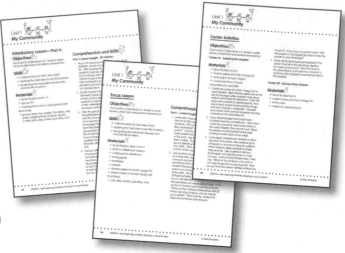

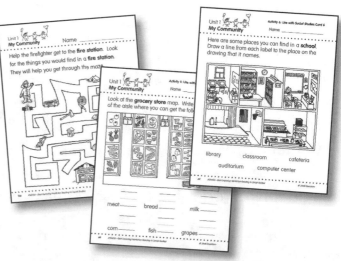

Research

Academic Readiness

The current thrust of education spending in the No Child Left Behind Act is academic readiness. This sweeping legislation places greater emphasis on language acquisition and early reading development in preschool and the primary grades. Research supports the belief that reading success by third grade leads to later academic success (U.S. Department of Education 2000).

Young children's early reading and writing proficiency is, therefore, an area of great interest both to policy makers and early-childhood professionals. The Early Reading First guidelines (U.S. Department of Education 2001) in No Child Left Behind include a program goal emphasizing the following:

- Oral language
- Phonological awareness
- Print awareness
- Alphabetic knowledge

A report from the National Institute of Child Health and Human Development, widely known as the Report of the National Reading Panel (2000), has generated new research in early reading. Despite the reading research base drawn on by the National Reading Panel, questions about young children's literacy development persist. How do children first begin to use written language? What can classroom teachers do to help all children be successful in unlocking the alphabetic principle and the code system of written language?

Early reading is an interwoven web of experiences, one part of which is children's early exposure to print in their world. Supplementing and enriching the curriculum with activities using familiar print provides an "auditory and visual anchor to remember letter symbol and sound" (Christie et al. 2002). By including activities with environmental print (the print found in a child's natural environment), teachers can provide opportunities for children to connect their prior knowledge to literacy experiences in school. Such experiences with familiar print assist children with word recognition and provide them with a sense of ownership when they recognize product logos and product labels that they see in their communities every day.

This book will guide the early childhood educator with a variety of ideas for enriching an existing comprehensive integrated curriculum for young children with environmental-print connections. You will find that encounters with environmental-print activities assist children in making connections between literacy experiences they encounter in their personal lives and those they learn at school.

Learning to Read

Early childhood educators have much to consider as they negotiate instructional strategies in their own classroom settings. Decades of research suggest that children start developing early literacy skills through their day-to-day experiences in a print-rich literate society (Berry 2001; Christie, Enz, and Vukelich 2002; Ferreiro and Teberosky 1982; Goodman 1986; Harste, Burke, and Woodward 1982). Children's prior knowledge of print in the environment—signs, billboards, logos, and functional print that saturate their world—can be used by teachers to make a meaningful bridge between what children already know and what they encounter in the school curriculum (Christie et al. 2002; Duke and Purcell-Gates 2003; Orellana and Hernandez 2003; Xu and Rutledge 2003).

Introduction

Research *(cont.)*

Purposeful planned encounters with environmental print can assist children in making connections between print in the home, print in the community, and school literacy experiences. Teachers can assist young children to become proficient readers and writers in many ways. The National Association for the Education of Young Children (2001) suggests the integrated use of speaking, listening, reading, and writing in the following ways:

- Provide social experiences for using language purposefully.
- Use reading and speaking to support oral language and vocabulary development.
- Use the home language and culture to introduce new words and concepts.
- Build on children's experiences.
- Provide opportunities to write.
- Play with language to develop phonemic awareness.
- Build knowledge of letters, sounds, and words.

This book provides opportunities for students to participate in all of these activities.

Simmons, Gunn, Smith, and Kame'enui (1994) stress the importance of teaching letters and sounds for reading success. They suggest the teaching of phonemic awareness through segmenting and blending sounds. While the awareness of sound units in phonemes, syllables, and words is a strong indicator of later reading success, keep in mind that, above all, reading is a meaning-making process. Letter and sound correspondences are beginning components of learning to read, but the comprehension of text is why children learn to read. The preteaching activities provide opportunities for students to work on phonemic awareness skills.

Satisfaction and enjoyment, the power of human interaction, the communication of important messages, pleasure and delight in the words themselves, along with the ability to match letters to sounds, overlay the skills of decoding. Phonemic awareness, the knowledge of rhyming, blending, and segmenting of letter sounds, serve as knowledge only if embedded in meaningful experiences. It is the responsibility of educators to provide meaningful experiences for students. As you complete the activities in this book with your students, you will be providing students with these meaningful experiences.

Refer to the References Cited (page 171) for a complete list of the sources used to create this book.

Best Practices: Learning to Read

Reading Readiness

All students need a good foundation in basic developmental areas such as language, cognition, motor development, social and emotional development, and self-help. Many early childhood classrooms include students with chronological ages from four to six years old. Developmentally, this could mean huge differences in readiness skills and abilities within one classroom. To help prepare all students for emergent reading and writing curriculums, certain objectives need to be taught when students first begin school.

Twelve of the reading-readiness objectives include the following:

1. Students recite their own name.

2. Students recognize their own names in writing.

3. Students demonstrate an understanding of left-to-right progression (moving hand and eyes across a page left to right).

4. Students understand the concepts of *same* and *different*.

5. Students match, sort, and classify objects, pictures, and shapes that have common properties.

6. Students understand rhyming words.

7. Students understand the concept of *opposite*.

8. Students understand the concept of *sequencing*.

9. Students can express themselves in complete sentences.

10. Students demonstrate phonemic awareness (understanding that sounds are the building blocks for our language).

11. Students can identify alphabet letters.

12. Students demonstrate phonics awareness (understanding that language sounds have written symbols).

The 12 objectives listed above are just some of the reading-readiness skills recommended as a foundation for an emergent, lifelong reader. Other factors that are as important include attention span, emotional maturity, and language experiences.

A well-balanced early childhood program includes many of these objectives and supports a learning environment enriched with literacy activities. *Start Exploring Nonfiction Reading in Social Studies* can assist teachers in providing this type of environment. Nonfiction text that stimulates language development and student participation can help children at all levels become beginning readers and writers. Since the lessons have already been prepared and organized, hours of teacher and parent preparation time can be used instead for important student guidance and teaching time.

Introduction

Best Practices:
Learning to Read (cont.)

Interactive Reading Steps

The following steps provide effective reading strategies to help students improve their reading skills.

Modeled Reading

When a teacher reads out loud with enthusiasm and fluency, this provides students with a modeled reading lesson. Students make predictions about the story being read, discuss together facts about the main characters and events, and share their own subject-related experiences. The purpose of this type of reading is to foster a desire to read. It also helps enrich students' vocabulary and enhances their knowledge of the world around them. It is recommended that both fiction and nonfiction be read aloud to students on a daily basis.

Shared Reading

During shared reading times, the teacher and students read together from the same book, song, or poem. Shared reading often involves repetition and helps students connect to stories in a nonthreatening atmosphere. Students increase their vocabulary and learn to problem-solve and predict in a group setting. Shared reading helps promote independent reading. Small mini-books that students create are also great tools to use for shared reading. All the books have the same words and are often related to the thematic unit being studied.

Guided Reading

During guided reading, the teacher works with students who are grouped by ability levels. The students read the same simple story and feel successful because the reading material has been chosen to meet their needs and abilities. In such groups, students build self-confidence by sharing information they read about and by successfully understanding the material they are reading. They answer problem-solving questions about the material and are given several opportunities to respond. Overall, these types of groups strengthen the students' thinking skills.

Independent Reading

During independent reading, students read materials for practice and enjoyment. They choose high-interest books that help promote fluency and responsibility for their own learning. In the beginning, these materials often contain simple text and repetitive language. Most of the books, poems, and charts for independent reading are texts the students have already been exposed to several times during the modeled-, shared-, and guided-reading sessions.

Best Practices:
Learning to Read *(cont.)*

Language Development

Long before students are introduced to written words, reading skills are being developed. Practicing oral language is a vital reading-readiness skill. There are several ways to bring excellent language development activities into a classroom environment. Here are some suggestions that could be used to enhance student vocabulary, self-esteem, and language acquisition:

- reading out loud to the students (nonfiction and fiction material)
- repetitive language in big books with student participation
- specific sharing times for students
- reciting poetry and singing thematic songs
- puppetry
- books with tapes at listening centers
- partner visiting times
- whole-class brainstorming sessions and discussions
- journal dictations
- "big buddy" activities (cross-age tutors)
- book sharing with "adopted grandparents"
- dramatization of short plays, poems, and stories
- monthly videotaping sessions
- dress-up area in the classroom
- student/teacher conversations
- storytelling
- class "visiting times" during centers or free play
- educational videos
- "Star (or Person) of the Week" sharing
- flag salute (explanation of words)

Introduction

Best Practices: The Five Components of Reading

The Report of the National Reading Panel marked a qualitative shift in beginning reading and writing instruction across the United States (National Institute of Child Health and Human Development 2000). It has generated new early reading standards, curriculum approaches, and classroom practices. The No Child Left Behind legislation has taken the outcomes of the National Reading Panel (NRP) report and translated these into very specific Reading First guidelines. These guidelines specify that instructional programs be based on valid scientific research and address the learning needs of all students, including high and low achievers, English language learners, and special education students. The guidelines further specify the five essential components in high-quality reading instruction that emerged from the Report of the National Reading Panel: 1. Phonemic Awareness, 2. Phonics, 3. Fluency, 4. Comprehension, 5. Vocabulary.

Phonemic awareness instruction should provide explicit instruction that focuses on letter-sound relationships, segmenting, and blending. The Reading First guidelines look for early linkage between sounds and letter symbols, even before letter names are learned, as well as ongoing assessment of phonemic awareness skills to inform instruction.

Phonics and word study instruction, according to the National Reading Panel, should also be explicit and systematic and teach letter-sound connections and blending skills to read whole words. These same skills must be applied to learning to spell. Reading text demands that students immediately apply their phonics knowledge to decode and comprehend what is being read. And, as with phonemic awareness instruction, phonics and word study skills must be systematically assessed to inform continued instruction.

Fluency instruction appears in the NRP report as an essential component of reading. The Reading First guidelines call for opportunities for oral repeated reading that is supported by the teacher, by peers, and at home by family members. The text that students read and reread should be well matched to their reading skills and should build rate and accuracy of oral reading.

Comprehension instruction, not surprisingly, appears in the NRP report as an essential component of reading instruction. This must include teaching before, during, and after reading both narrative and informational text. Teachers must explicitly explain and model strategies that aid comprehension. Discussion techniques and questioning strategies must also be directly explained and modeled by the teacher. Extended opportunities must be provided to struggling readers—low readers, English language learners, and special-needs students—to participate in successful reading experiences.

Vocabulary instruction is the fifth component of the NRP report. Vocabulary instruction, according to Reading First guidelines, must also be direct, systematic, and explicit. The meanings of words and word-learning strategies must be taught by the teacher. Structural analysis of words and the etymology of words must be taught as well.

Best Practices: The Five Components of Reading *(cont.)*

Phonemic Awareness

Phonemic awareness refers to a person's ability to attend to and manipulate the sounds of spoken words. In order to begin reading, a child needs to understand that words are made up of individual sounds. As described in the Report of the National Reading Panel, there are several elements involved in phonemic awareness instruction. These include phoneme isolation, phoneme identification, phoneme categorization, phoneme blending, phoneme segmentation, phoneme deletion, phoneme addition, and phoneme substitution. This book provides lessons and activities to draw attention to the sounds that make up words. Students need to have a strong understanding of the spoken language before they can understand the written language. Sounds are the building blocks of language. Students must first have phonemic awareness before phonics can make sense to them. There is first an awareness of spoken words, then syllables, onsets, and rimes. The definitions below are important for any teacher or parent to understand when working with students at the early childhood level.

- *Phonemic awareness* is being able to hear the sounds that make up words, see relationships between these sounds, and create or rearrange sounds to create new words.
- *Phoneme* is an individual sound; for example, "t" is a phoneme and so is "ow."
- *Onset* is the beginning sound or sounds before the first vowel. In *cat* "c" is the onset. In *stop* "st" is the onset.
- *Rime* is the first vowel and the rest of the word. The rime in *man* is "an." The rime in *stand* is "and."

- *Phonics* is the process of associating sounds with written symbols. Phonics gives students word attack skills for sounding out and blending letter sounds in written words.

Note: Both phonemic awareness and phonics are needed to help students develop word recognition skills.

A balanced literacy approach combines phonemic awareness, phonics, sight words, vocabulary development, comprehension, and fluency into an enriched learning environment for emergent readers and authors. Students themselves help to create such an environment by using natural and functional written language. For example, students may help dictate "Rules for Taking Care of Our Pet Fish." There might also be a post office in the classroom where students can draw pictures and write letters to each other. A content rich environment integrates science, social studies, math, and the arts to make learning more meaningful for students.

Phonemic Awareness Activities

Thumbs Up, Thumbs Down (Identifying Identical and Differing Phoneme Structures)

Tell students you are going to say two words. If the two are the same word, students should show thumbs up. If the two are not the same word, students should show thumbs down. Demonstrate several words for the students until they understand the task. For example, if you said the words *cap – cap*, students should indicate they are the same word by showing thumbs up. If you said the words *cap – tap*, students should indicate they are not the same word by showing thumbs down.

Introduction

Best Practices: The Five Components of Reading *(cont.)*

Phoneme Count (Counting Phonemes)

Students are to determine how many sounds they hear in a word and then clap one time for each sound. For example, if you say the word *sun*, students should determine there are three sounds and clap three times.

If students have difficulty determining the number of sounds, help them analyze the word by segmenting it. For example, after saying the word *sun*, segment the word by saying /s/ pause /u/ pause /n/. In this way, students will have an easier time determining the different sounds.

Mystery Word (Phoneme Blending)

Say a mystery word by saying one sound at a time. When all the sounds have been made, students are to blend the sounds together to tell the mystery word. Begin by providing an example so students know what is expected. For example, if the mystery word is *big*, say, /b/ pause /i/ pause /g/. Students should identify that the mystery word is *big*. If students have a difficult time, model saying the three sounds of the word again several times, each time with shorter pauses until the word sounds like normal speech.

As students demonstrate their understanding of the activity and their capability to blend, use mystery words with more sounds. For example, expand from words like *bat* to words such as *bend* and *bust*.

Use nonsense words as mystery words, too. Nonsense words are words that we do not use in the English language. An example of a nonsense word is *bip*. By using nonsense words, you can informally assess how well students understand the concept of blending.

The Same Sound (Phoneme Isolation)

List three words that begin with the same sound. Have students identify the sound they hear at the beginning of the words. For example, if you say *hen*, *hand*, and *hop*, students should indicate the beginning sound is /h/.

Alternatively, have the students identify the ending sound of three words. For example, if you say *sip*, *cop*, and *map*, students should indicate that they hear /p/ at the end of all three words.

Starts the Same (Phoneme Categorization)

Read a list of three words in succession, two of which begin with the same sound. Have students name the two words from the list that begin with the same sound. For example, have students listen for the /p/ sound. Say the words *pin*, *dog*, and *pat*. Students should indicate that the words *pin* and *pat* begin with the /p/ sound. Alternatively, the students may name the word that does not begin with /p/.

Target Sound (Phoneme Categorization)

Determine a list of words, about half of which begin with the targeted sound and half of which begin with other sounds. Say the words, one at a time. If the word begins with the targeted sound, students perform a prespecified activity or gesture. If the word does not begin with the sound, students do nothing. For example, if the target sound is /b/, students can buzz around the room when you say the word *baby*. If the word is *run*, students do nothing.

Best Practices: The Five Components of Reading *(cont.)*

Break It Down (Phoneme Segmentation)

Tell students you are going to say a word. They are to break the word apart or segment the word by saying each sound they hear, one sound at a time. For example, if you say the word *hat*, students should say /h/ pause /a/ pause /t/. Begin by modeling several examples for students.

Alliteration Sentences

Emphasize words that begin with the same sound by having students think of sentences in which all or most of the words begin with the same sound. For example, if students are learning about the /s/ sound, the following sentence could be made: *Sam sees a silly snake.* This activity can be done orally, or the sentence can be written down and students can illustrate a picture to correspond with the sentence.

First or Last (Phoneme Isolation)

Fold 3" x 5" index cards in half in order to create two 3" x 2.5" boxes. Draw a line on the fold to better differentiate the boxes. Provide each student with an index card and a manipulative such as a bear counter, a penny, or an eraser. Practice naming the sections of the card with students. For example, ask students to place their manipulative in the first box. Tell students that this is the beginning box because it is first. Ask students to place their manipulative in the second box. Tell students that this is the ending box because it is last. Be sure students understand the name and purpose of the two boxes before proceeding to the next step.

Determine the sound for which you want students to listen. Create a list of words, several of which have the determined sound at the beginning of the word, and several of which

have the sound at the end of the word. For example, if the sound you want students to listen for is /s/, use a list similar to the following:

Begins with /s/		Ends with /s/	
sit	soap	rice	cats
sag	salt	rocks	prince

Say a word from the list. If students hear /s/ at the beginning of the word, students should slide their manipulative onto the first or beginning box on the index card. If students hear /s/ at the end of the word, they should slide their manipulative onto the second or last box on the index card. If the word is *sad*, students should slide their manipulative into the first or beginning box because /s/ is at the beginning of the word. If the word is *pots*, students should slide their manipulative onto the ending or last box because /s/ is at the end of the word. Demonstrate and practice several examples with students until they understand what is expected.

Alternatively, make "First or Last" a movement activity by placing two pieces of paper on the floor in front of a student. Play the game in the same way. Say a word such as *sit*. If the student hears the /s/ sound at the beginning of the word, the student jumps or steps on the piece of paper that is on the left. If the word is *cats*, the student jumps or steps on the piece of paper on the right, because the /s/ sound is at the end of the word.

Introduction

Best Practices: The Five Components of Reading *(cont.)*

Rhyme Time

Say two words. If the words rhyme, students should perform one action. If the two words do not rhyme, students should perform another action. For example, say two words from the list below in succession. Have students indicate by smiling if the words rhyme. If the words do not rhyme, students should frown.

hot – dot   rhyme (smile)

ham – dog   do not rhyme (frown)

Once students demonstrate a good understanding of rhyming, an extension of the rhyming activity above is for the students to generate the two words. The teacher can then smile or frown in order to show if the words rhyme or do not rhyme. This is an excellent informal assessment. By monitoring the words the students provide, a combination of rhyming words and non-rhyming words, the teacher will be able to assess students' understanding.

Three Rhymes in a Row

Tell students you are going to say two words that rhyme. Students need to generate a third word that rhymes with the two you said. For example, if you say the words *pat* and *hat*, students might say the word *cat*. Repeat the three words in order to emphasize the rhyme.

They Rhyme

Read a list of three words in succession. The three words should include two words that rhyme and one word that does not rhyme. Students should determine which two words rhyme. For example, the teacher may say *cat*, *bet*, *mat*. Students should indicate that the words *cat* and *mat* rhyme.

Fluency

Fluency is the ability to read quickly and accurately while at the same time using good oral expression, proper phrasing, and appropriate pacing. Fluency is particularly important for young children who are just learning to read or struggling readers, or children learning English as a second language. These students expend too much cognitive energy decoding words letter by letter, thereby losing understanding of the material. Their attention and energy is focused on getting each sound correct rather than finding meaning and making sense of the text. This is clear when, after listening to a struggling reader, the student does not understand what has just been read. Children who read more fluently use their cognitive energy and attention to focus on the meaning of the print. They comprehend what they read. The fluent reader has enough attention in reserve to make connections between the text and their own background knowledge, which gives the reader a deeper understanding of the material. When oral reading of text is more fluent and sounds like natural speech, children are better able to pull from their own prior knowledge and background experiences for comprehension.

Building Comprehension

Good readers are taught to use a wide array of strategies to make sense of what they are reading. They are explicitly taught to make connections as they read by using their prior knowledge as well as their visualizing, inferring, and synthesizing skills.

Best Practices: The Five Components of Reading *(cont.)*

Good readers ask questions before they read, as they read, and after they read. Street signs, cereal boxes, and billboards all provide opportunities for readers to interact with words in a meaningful, purposeful way.

This book provides a variety of lessons and activities that will assist you with creative ideas for repeated readings for building fluency and developing comprehension. The lessons are designed to look beyond the color and context clues of environmental print to read words. A variety of writing activities and ways to reinforce making meaning during reading are provided, as well as ways to scaffold the development of comprehension strategies.

Building Vocabulary

Opportunities abound within the typical classroom for children to learn new vocabulary and to experiment with words. To learn new words, children must experience words in frequent, meaningful, and varied contexts. The more exposure a child has to words, the better able he or she is to read and comprehend. Vocabulary knowledge, then, is an important factor in reading comprehension.

Sight words are those high-frequency words that do not necessarily decode and that must be read with automaticity by children. The lessons in this book provide oral-reading opportunities for children of varying reading levels and different learning styles in a whole-class setting or in a small-group setting. The lessons and activities reinforce the sight words that children must recognize automatically. Sight words are repeated to develop visual memory and improve visual-auditory perception.

Vocabulary learning is comprised of roughly four stages: listening, speaking, reading, and writing. Children develop these components of vocabulary in this sequence as well. A child's first vocabulary is the listening vocabulary. Children arrive at school with a receptive vocabulary of thousands and thousands of words. Speaking vocabulary develops after the listening vocabulary. Reading and writing vocabulary begin expanding dramatically after the age of five or six. For very young children, the first words learned are those that are experienced within the home, family, and care-giving environments. As children interact with their environment, they construct and learn concepts for which words become labels. The environment for young children includes experiences with words on products, packaging, signs, and billboards.

Following basic principles for developing vocabulary with young children, the subsequent lesson plans address the following:

- teach useful words that young children will likely encounter.
- teach words that are conceptually related to others.
- teach words that relate to their background knowledge.
- generate an enthusiasm for and interest in words.

Introduction

Best Practices: Differentiation

Over the past few years, classrooms have evolved into diverse pools of learners. Gifted students, English language learners, learning-disabled students, high achievers, underachievers, and average students all come together to learn from one teacher. The teacher is expected to meet their diverse needs in one classroom. It brings back memories of the one-room schoolhouse from early American history. Not too long ago, lessons were designed to be one-size-fits-all. It was thought that students in the same grade level learned in similar ways. Today we know that viewpoint is faulty. Students have differing learning styles, come from different cultures, experience a variety of emotions, and have varied interests. For each subject, they also differ in academic readiness. At times, the challenges teachers face can be overwhelming. They struggle to figure out how to create learning environments that address the differences they find in their students.

What is differentiation? Carol Ann Tomlinson of the University of Virginia says, "Differentiation is simply a teacher attending to the learning needs of a particular student or small group of students, rather than teaching a class as though all individuals in it were basically alike" (2000). Differentiation can be accomplished by any teacher who keeps the learners at the forefront of his or her instruction. The effective teacher asks, "What am I going to do to shape instruction to meet the needs of all my learners?" One method or methodology will not reach all students.

Differentiation encompasses what is taught, how it is taught, and the products students create to show what they have learned. When differentiating curriculum, teachers become the organizers of learning opportunities within the classroom environment. These categories are often referred to as *content, process*, and *product*.

- **Content:** Differentiating the content means putting more depth into the curriculum by organizing the curriculum concepts and structure of knowledge.
- **Process:** Differentiating the process requires the use of varied instructional techniques and materials to enhance students' learning.
- **Product:** When products are differentiated, cognitive development and students' abilities to express themselves improves.

Why Should We Differentiate?

The more we understand how students learn, the more we understand why curriculum needs to be differentiated. Students make meaning out of what is taught in classrooms based on their prior understandings, learning styles, attitudes, and beliefs. Differentiated curriculum takes these into account. Research has shown that students need to be pushed just a little beyond their independence levels for real learning to take place (Csikszentmihalyi 1990). Differentiated curriculum provides an avenue by which lessons can challenge, but not overwhelm, students based on their ability levels. Both emotions and movement enhance the learning process and when students have the opportunity to study their interests, their motivation for learning increases (Piaget 1978). A differentiated classroom takes interests into account. Finally, we know that everyone learns in a variety of ways. Curriculum that is differentiated allows for a variety of grouping techniques and assignments so that teachers can reach students regardless of their backgrounds.

Best Practices:
Differentiation *(cont.)*

Teachers should differentiate content, process, and product according to students' characteristics. These characteristics include students' readiness, learning styles, and interests.

- **Readiness:** If a learning experience matches closely with students' previous skills and understanding of a topic, they will learn better.

- **Learning styles:** Teachers should create assignments that allow students to complete work according to their personal preferences and styles.

- **Interests:** If a topic sparks excitement in the students, then they will become involved in learning and better remember what is taught.

How to Begin Differentiating

As previously discussed, differentiation encompasses content, process, and product. Below are some specific ways in which teachers can differentiate within these three categories.

Teachers can differentiate content by:
- reading an excerpt of an article, as opposed to the entire article.
- reading shorter chunks of text over a longer period of time.

Teachers can differentiate process by:
- grouping students in different ways: whole class, teacher-directed groups, independent groups, partners, or individuals.
- providing scaffolds for students to be able to meet the expectations.
- breaking steps down into smaller parts to make each step more manageable.
- preteaching more difficult skills, vocabulary, or concepts prior to a whole-class lesson.

- having students read independently or with the teacher, depending on their reading level.

Teachers can differentiate product by allowing students to:

- create a photo collage versus a hand-drawn illustration.
- give an oral presentation versus a written presentation.
- choose a product that best fits their interests and strengths.

To make the activities within this book most effective, teachers should differentiate the lessons whenever possible. Not all students need to be engaged in exactly the same activity at the same time. The various activities included in this book provide opportunities for differentiating instruction within the lessons. Look for the heading "Time to Differentiate!" and the suggestions that are provided under this heading. You will find strategies for differentiating the lessons when preteaching each card as well as in each focus lesson. Strategies for differentiating instruction are given for above-level students, below-level students, and English learners. See the following page for specific strategies for supporting English language learners.

Introduction

Correlation to Standards *(cont.)*

Standard	Objective	Lesson and Page Number
Standard 5 Uses the general skills and strategies of the reading process	**(K–2) 5.1** Uses mental images based on pictures and print to aid in comprehension of text	Unit 3 Lesson A (page 120)
	(Pre-K) 5.3 Understands that illustrations and pictures convey meaning	Unit 3 Lesson A (page 120)
	(Pre-K) 5.11 Uses emergent reading skills to "read" a story (e.g., gathers meaning from words and pictures)	Unit 2 Lesson B (page 90) Unit 4 Lesson B (page 158)
	(Pre-K) 5.13 Uses visual and verbal cues, including pictures, to comprehend new words and stories	Unit 2 Lesson A (page 84)
Standard 6 Uses reading skills and strategies to understand and interpret a variety of literary texts	**(K–2) 6.4** Knows the main idea or theme of a story	Unit 2 Lesson A (page 84)
	(Pre-K) 6.5 Relates stories to his/her own life experience	Unit 1 Lesson A (page 42) Unit 1 Lesson B (page 48) Unit 3 Lesson B (page 126) Unit 4 Lesson A (page 152)
	(K–2) 6.5 Relates stories to personal experiences (e.g., events, characters, conflicts, themes)	Unit 1 Lesson A (page 42) Unit 4 Lesson A (page 152)

Correlation to Standards *(cont.)*

Standard	Objective	Lesson and Page Number
Standard 7 Uses reading skills and strategies to understand and interpret a variety of informational texts	(K–2) 7.1 Uses reading skills and strategies to understand a variety of informational texts (e.g., written directions, signs, captions, warning labels, informational books)	Unit 4 Lesson B (page 158)
	(K–2) 7.2 Understands the main idea and supporting details of simple expository information	Unit 1 Lesson B (page 48)
	(K–2) 7.3 Summarizes information found in texts (e.g., retells in own words)	Unit 2 Lesson B (page 90)
	(K–2) 7.4 Relates new information to prior knowledge and experience	Unit 3 Lesson B (page 126)

My Community

Community Workers

Kinds of Land and Water

The United States

Introduction to Unit 1: My Community

My Community is a great theme for younger students. It is readily accessible, and students will be able to use prior knowledge to discuss and comprehend the reading passages. Key vocabulary terms such as *fire station, neighborhood, hospital, doctors, nurses,* and *post office* are introduced. Students will learn to apply nonfiction material to real-life situations. In this unit, students will also learn to recognize proposition and support.

Skills Taught in This Unit

- understanding the main idea of text
- applying the main idea to real-life situations
- recognizing the connection between text and real-life situations
- identifying proposition statements
- identifying support statements
- recognizing proposition and support in text

Directions for the Teacher

You have many different options when teaching this unit. You can use the nonfiction text pages (Social Studies Cards) and teach the content using the strategies that precede each text passage. Or, you can teach nonfiction skills and strategies by teaching the whole unit, starting with the introductory lesson, then teaching the focus lesson, and then following up with the center activities. This format repeats for the second lesson in the unit. Conclude the unit by teaching the wrap-up activity to tie all the nonfiction text and skills together.

Unit 1
My Community

fire station

Activating Prior Knowledge

Show students Social Studies Card 1. Ask them to describe what they see. Ask them to tell you what they see in the picture, who the person is, and where they think the picture was taken. If possible, arrange for a fire truck to come and visit your school the same day you discuss this card. The firefighters will usually do a short presentation about fire safety and give students a tour of the truck. Ask students if any of their parents are firefighters or if they know a firefighter. Ask them to share any experiences they may have had visiting a fire station. Ask students to think about why being a firefighter is so important. Students should share their thoughts on this topic. Ask students to brainstorm all the things that firefighters do. Make a list of these jobs on the board.

Language Development

Show students the card. Ask them to describe what they see in the picture. Tell them that the words at the top of the card say *fire station*. Ask them to look at the first word, *fire*. Ask them to tell you what the word *fire* begins with. After they respond, ask them to practice making the /f/ sound. Tell them to look at the word *station*. Explain that even though it begins with the letter "s," the first two letters work together to make the beginning sound. Tell them that when two letters work together to make a sound, we call that a *blend*. Have students practice making the /st/ blend. Direct students' attention to the sentence at the bottom of the card. Ask them if they recognize any words in the sentence. While pointing to the words, read the sentence aloud. Ask students to read the sentence with you while you point to the words. Individual students can point to the words while the rest of the class reads the sentence.

Building Knowledge and Comprehension

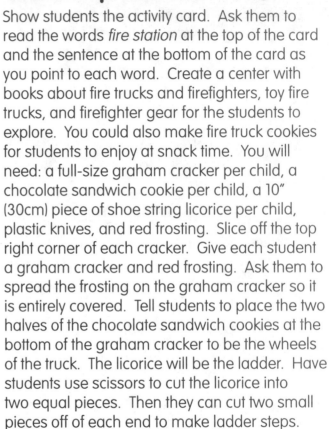

Show students the activity card. Ask them to read the words *fire station* at the top of the card and the sentence at the bottom of the card as you point to each word. Create a center with books about fire trucks and firefighters, toy fire trucks, and firefighter gear for the students to explore. You could also make fire truck cookies for students to enjoy at snack time. You will need: a full-size graham cracker per child, a chocolate sandwich cookie per child, a 10" (30cm) piece of shoe string licorice per child, plastic knives, and red frosting. Slice off the top right corner of each cracker. Give each student a graham cracker and red frosting. Ask them to spread the frosting on the graham cracker so it is entirely covered. Tell students to place the two halves of the chocolate sandwich cookies at the bottom of the graham cracker to be the wheels of the truck. The licorice will be the ladder. Have students use scissors to cut the licorice into two equal pieces. Then they can cut two small pieces off of each end to make ladder steps.

Time to Differentiate!

For English language learners, build their background knowledge prior to the lessons. Show students the card. Point to various things in the picture and name them. Ask students to repeat the words. Write those words on sticky notes and place them on the picture.

For below-level students, preview the card in a small group. Read the words at the top of the card and ask students to repeat them. While pointing to each word, read the sentence at the bottom of the card. Repeat this several times.

fire station

The **fire station** is a safe place to go in your neighborhood.

Activating Prior Knowledge

Show students Social Studies Card 2. Ask them to look closely at the picture and tell you what they see. Ask them if the park in the picture looks like a park that they go to. Ask students to describe the park that they visit. Ask them questions such as the following: Is there a lot of grass? Are there swings and slides? Ask students to name their favorite things to do at the park. Share an experience you had at a park when you were younger. If possible, take students on a walking field trip to the nearest park. While at the park, decide as a class what piece of equipment is the most fun to play on. After returning to class, have students discuss the equipment they would like to have at a park. Create a Word Bank on the board with students' ideas. Have students draw pictures of their ideal parks and label the parts of their pictures.

Language Development

Show students the card. Ask them to describe again what they see in the picture. Tell them to look at the word *park* at the top of the card. Ask them what the word *park* begins with. After they respond, practice making the /p/ sound. Ask them if they recognize the sound they hear at the end of the word. Practice making the /k/ sound. Write the word *park* on the board with the "p" separated from the "-ark." Explain that you are going to create new words that rhyme with the word *park* by changing the beginning sound. Ask students to help you create new words such as *dark*, *lark*, *bark*, and *mark*. Direct students' attention to the sentence at the bottom of the page. Ask them if they recognize any words in the sentence. While pointing to the words, read the sentence. Ask students to read the sentence with you while you point to the words.

Building Knowledge and Comprehension

Show students the card. Ask them to describe what they see. Ask them to read the word *park* at the top of the card as you point to it. Ask them to read the sentence at the bottom of the card as you point to each word. Ask students to brainstorm things they like to do at the park. Make a list of these ideas on the board or on chart paper. Read through the list with students, pointing to each word as you read it. Give each student a sheet of construction paper. Ask students to draw a picture of their favorite thing to do at a park. Model for the class first by drawing your favorite thing to do at a park. After students draw their pictures, ask them to complete the following sentence underneath their pictures: "At the park, I like to _____." Bind all the pages together into a class book that can be enjoyed all year long.

Time to Differentiate!

For English language learners, help them complete their sentences in the Building Knowledge and Comprehension lesson. After students have drawn their pictures of their favorite things to do at the park, label their picture. Then encourage each student to use the label to complete his or her sentence.

For below-level students, practice identifying the beginning and ending sounds of the word *park*. If needed, tell students what each sound is and have them repeat the sound after you. Name other words that begin with the letter "p," and have students repeat the words, emphasizing the /p/ sound at the beginning.

park

You can play in the **park**.

Unit 1
My Community

post office

Activating Prior Knowledge

Show students Social Studies Card 3. Ask them to look at the card closely and describe what they see. Ask them to share what they already know about the post office. Ask students what a post office is for and why it is important that we have post offices. Ask students to think about how a letter gets from place to place. Discuss how we mail letters and how the post office sorts them. The letter travels by truck or air to its destination city and another post office in that city where it is sorted again. The letter is then taken by a mail carrier and delivered to its final destination, possibly a business or a home. Read any books you may have in your classroom library about the post office or mail carriers. If possible, take a trip to the nearest post office.

Language Development

Show students the card. Ask them to describe again what they see in the picture. Tell them to look at the words *post office* at the top of the card. Ask them what the word *post* begins with. After they respond, ask them to practice the /p/ sound. Ask them to listen closely as you say the word and see if they recognize the sounds they hear at the end of the word *post*. Ask them to practice making the /st/ blend. Discuss with students the word *office*. Point out the letter "c" and how it makes the soft "c" sound /s/ in the word *office*. Help students to think of more soft "c" words. List them on the board. Tell students that when "c" is followed by "e," "i," or "y" it makes the /s/ sound. Now direct students' attention to the sentence at the bottom of the page. Tell them to look carefully and see if they recognize any words in the sentence. While pointing to the words, read the sentence to students. Ask students to read the sentence with you while you point to the words.

Building Knowledge and Comprehension

Show students the card. Ask them to describe what they see. Ask them to read the words *post office* at the top of the card as you point to them. Ask them to read the sentence at the bottom of the card as you point to each word. Discuss with students how we follow a certain form when we write letters. As a class, write a letter to the school principal about the post office. Put a pretend stamp on it and mail it at the school office. Explain to the principal ahead of time what you are doing and ask him or her to respond. If possible, ask the local mail carrier to come to school and tell the class about his or her job. If a parent of a student in class is a mail carrier, invite that parent to talk to the class. Set up a post office center in the classroom where students can write each other letters. Each week, designate a different student as the mail carrier, and have him or her deliver the class mail.

Time to Differentiate!

For English language learners, scaffold the letter-writing activity in the Building Knowledge and Comprehension lesson. Ask students to help you write a letter as a group. Say each sentence you are composing and have students repeat it before writing it on a large sheet of paper. Let each student sign it.

For below-level students, scaffold the letter-writing activity in the Building Knowledge and Comprehension lesson. Create a template for the letter with parts of the letter already written. Leave blanks for students to fill in. Write words on the board to help students complete their letters.

post office

Mail is sorted at the **post office**.

grocery store

Activating Prior Knowledge

Show students Social Studies Card 4. Ask them to describe what they see in the picture. Talk about grocery stores in general and how lucky we are to have them. Discuss with students how some countries do not have grocery stores and how people have to wait in line just to get simple things like water, rice, and flour. Ask students to share their experiences with going to the grocery store. Ask them questions such as the following: Do you go with your dad or mom, brother or sister? Do you help put things in the cart? Ask students to think about the different departments in the grocery store such as the bakery, deli, meat department, produce department, and frozen-food section. Ask them to think about why some things are refrigerated or frozen and others are not. Ask students what we call the person who we pay for the food we buy (the checker). If possible, take a field trip to the nearest grocery store.

Language Development

Ask students to look at the card. Tell them the large words at the top of the card say *grocery store*. Ask them to read them with you while you point to the words. Now direct students' attention to the sentence at the bottom of the page. Ask them if they recognize any words in the sentence. While pointing to the words, read the sentence. Ask students to read the sentence with you while you point to the words. Tell students that you need their help in making a grocery list. Ask them to think of things one might see at a grocery store. Write their ideas on the board. Review the word list with students. Call on them individually or as a group to say the words on the list. Remind students to think about the beginning, middle, and ending sounds in each word.

Building Knowledge and Comprehension

Show students the card and ask them to describe what they see. Ask them to read the words *grocery store* at the top of the card as you point to them. Ask them to read the sentence at the bottom of the card as you point to each word. Provide a grocery store center for students to visit in class. Include in the center a toy cash register and play money, shelves with products on them, empty boxes of food that students bring from home (like cereal boxes and boxes of pasta), plastic fruits and vegetables, and a toy grocery cart. Tell students that when they visit the center they must have a job as either the shopper, the checker, or the grocery store department worker. Provide paper and pencils in the center for students to create grocery lists. Also, bring in coupons clipped from the newspaper for students to use.

Time to Differentiate!

For English language learners, scaffold the list-making activity in the Language Development lesson. Ask students to help you write a list as a group. Let each student draw a picture of what he or she would like on the list. Have each student paste or glue the drawing onto a sheet of chart paper. Then write the word for each item on the list.

For below-level students, scaffold the list-making activity in the Building Knowledge and Comprehension lesson. Ask students to draw each item on their lists. Then have each student name each item. Write the word for each item in highlighter marker so that students can trace over the letters.

grocery store

People buy food in a **grocery store**.

Unit 1
My Community

hospital

Activating Prior Knowledge

Show students Social Studies Card 5. Ask them to describe what they see. Where was the picture taken? Who are the people in the picture and what are they doing? Talk about how a hospital is part of the community, and the people who work there are called community helpers. Ask students if any of them have ever had to go to the hospital, either for an emergency or to visit a friend. Have students share their personal experiences. Talk about the stethoscopes the doctors wear around their necks and what they do. Borrow a stethoscope so students can take turns listening to each other's heartbeats. Talk about the different areas of the hospital and how each area is important for different reasons. For example, the radiology department is important because when people break bones, x-rays are taken there.

Language Development

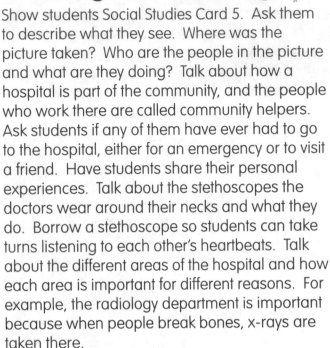

Show students the card again. Ask them to describe what they see in the picture. Tell students to look at the word at the top of the card. Ask them what they think the word is. Tell them the word is *hospital* and ask them to read it with you while you point to it. Then read it again, stretching the word out, "h-o-s-p-i-t-a-l." Tell students that the word *hospital* begins with the letter "h." Ask them to practice making the /h/ sound. Tell them the letter "h" makes a sound like a dog makes when it pants to keep cool. Tell them to stick out their tongues and pretend to pant like a dog while they make the /h/ sound. Now direct students' attention to the sentence at the bottom of the page. Ask them if they recognize any words in the sentence. While pointing to the words, read the sentence. Ask students to read the sentence with you while you point to the words.

Building Knowledge and Comprehension

Show students the card and ask them to describe what they see. Ask them to read the word *hospital* at the top of the card as you point to it. Ask them to read the sentence at the bottom of the card as you point to each word. Tell students to clap their hands when they read the word *hospital*. Provide a drama center with items that a doctor or nurse would wear or use. Some examples are the following: scrubs, doctor's coat, nurse's uniform, bandages, pillows, blankets, and a doctor's kit. Provide pretend prescription pads for students to write prescriptions. Choose a few students to help you model a scenario for the rest of the class. For example, "Beth is feeling sad today. Doctor Loren and Nurse Steve are going to help her feel better. The doctor listens to Beth's heart and decides that Beth needs to be cheered up. The doctor writes her a prescription for jellybeans and the nurse gives her the prescription." Make the center fun and simple.

Time to Differentiate!

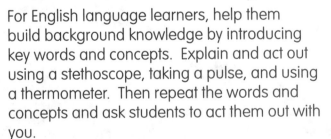

For English language learners, help them build background knowledge by introducing key words and concepts. Explain and act out using a stethoscope, taking a pulse, and using a thermometer. Then repeat the words and concepts and ask students to act them out with you.

For below-level students, scaffold the discussion activities by encouraging them to talk with partners before sharing their thoughts or experiences with the class. If needed, model for them how to answer in complete sentences.

hospital

Doctors and nurses work in a **hospital**.

Activating Prior Knowledge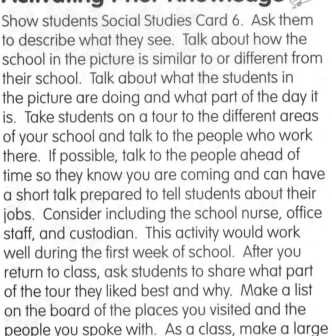

Show students Social Studies Card 6. Ask them to describe what they see. Talk about how the school in the picture is similar to or different from their school. Talk about what the students in the picture are doing and what part of the day it is. Take students on a tour to the different areas of your school and talk to the people who work there. If possible, talk to the people ahead of time so they know you are coming and can have a short talk prepared to tell students about their jobs. Consider including the school nurse, office staff, and custodian. This activity would work well during the first week of school. After you return to class, ask students to share what part of the tour they liked best and why. Make a list on the board of the places you visited and the people you spoke with. As a class, make a large wall map of the school. Label each part.

Language Development

Show students the card. Tell them to look at the word *school* at the top of the card. Ask them what the word *school* begins with. After they respond, ask them to practice the "sch" blend. Ask them to listen closely as you say the word and see if they recognize the sound they hear at the end of the word *school*. Ask them to practice making the /l/ sound. Write the word *school* on the board with the "sch" separated from the "-ool." Ask students to help you create new words that rhyme with the word *school* by changing the beginning sound. Examples include *pool, cool, drool, fool,* and *tool*. Now direct their attention to the sentence at the bottom of the page. Ask them if they recognize any words in the sentence. While pointing to the words, read the sentence. Ask students to read the sentence with you. Have students clap their hands when they hear the word *school*.

Building Knowledge and Comprehension

Show students the card. Ask them to describe what they see. Ask them to read the word *school* at the top of the card as you point to it. Ask them to read the sentence at the bottom of the card as you point to each word. Tell students to think about where their home is in relation to the school. Show students a map of your city. Tell them that you are going to give them a sheet of paper and you would like them to draw a map showing how to get from their house to the school. Model this activity first on a large scale in front of students. Show them how to draw streets, buildings, and intersections. Ask students to label each part of their maps. Have students draw a picture of their favorite thing at school. Ask students to complete this sentence frame on their drawings: "The thing I like best at school is _____." Bind the pages together into a class book.

Time to Differentiate!

For English language learners, preview the card and build students' vocabulary for the lesson. Point to and label the various people and things in the picture. Then say each word and have a student point to that person or thing on the card.

For below-level students, scaffold the writing activity. Write the sentence frame on the board. Model several ways to complete the sentence. Guide students in completing the sentence frame orally before having them do so in writing.

school

School is where kids go to learn.
Does your school look like this?

Unit 1
My Community
neighborhood

Activating Prior Knowledge

Show students Social Studies Card 7. Ask them to look at the card and describe what they see. Make a list on the board of what students see in the picture. Tell students to notice what is similar and different about the houses. How is this neighborhood similar to or different from the neighborhood that surrounds your school? Ask students to notice the power lines and streetlights in the picture. Are there power lines and streetlights in the neighborhood surrounding your school? Ask students to close their eyes and visualize the street that they live on. What do they see? What do the houses or apartments look like? Are they two stories? Are they close together or far apart? Are there stores or neighborhood pools? Spend this time talking with students about what makes a neighborhood and what the neighborhood they live in is like. Share what type of neighborhood you live in.

Language Development

Show students the card. Ask them to look at the word at the top of the card. Tell them that the word is *neighborhood* and have them read it with you while you point to it. Ask them to practice making the /n/ sound. Now direct students' attention to the sentence at the bottom of the page. Ask them if they recognize any words in the sentence. While pointing to the words, read the sentence. Ask students to read the sentence with you while you point to the words. Ask students to wave when they read the word *neighborhood*. Ask students to look at the list of words you developed in the Activating Prior Knowledge lesson. Use the words to create sentences with students. For example, "There are power lines above ground and houses with lots of windows in the neighborhood."

Building Knowledge and Comprehension

Show students the card and ask them to describe what they see. Ask them to read the word *neighborhood* at the top of the card as you point to it. Read the sentence at the bottom of the card. Ask students to tell you any words they recognize. Ask them to read the sentence at the bottom of the card as you point to each word. Read the sentence several times as a group. Tell students that together you are going to draw a map of their neighborhood. Ask students to tell you where to add things like streetlights, stop signs, streets, and other buildings that they pass. When the map is complete, ask students to share their ideas about what other things they would like to see in their neighborhood.

Time to Differentiate!

For English language learners, preteach the vocabulary needed for the Building Knowledge and Comprehension lesson. Show students pictures of a streetlight, stop sign, street, etc. Say each word as you show the picture, and then ask students to repeat it.

For below-level students, help them extend their sentences in the Language Development lesson. Begin by stating a simple sentence. Then encourage students to help you add words to extend the sentence and add more detail.

neighborhood

People live, work, and play
in a **neighborhood**.

museum

Activating Prior Knowledge

Show students Social Studies Card 8. Ask them to describe what they see in the picture. Tell students that the picture was taken in a museum and ask if they know what a museum is. Ask them to think about what all the bones in the picture were put together to make. Ask students if they know where the bones came from and who put them together. Tell students that when scientists find the fossilized bones, the bones are then taken back to a museum, cleaned, and put together like a puzzle. Ask students what they think a museum is. Ask them to think about why we have museums. Talk with students about the different kinds of museums a person could visit—art, science, nature, history, and state museums. Ask students to share any experiences they may have had at museums. Talk about the museums that are in your area.

Language Development

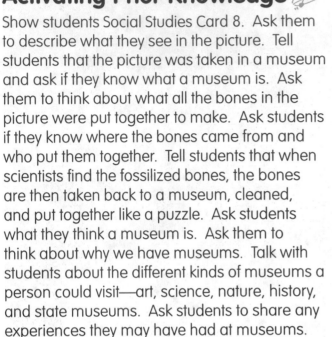

Show students the card again. Ask them to describe what they see in the picture. Tell students to look at the word at the top of the card. Ask them what they think the word is. Tell them to look at the picture for a clue. Tell them the word is *museum* and ask them to read it with you while you point to it. Then read it again, stretching out the word, "m-u-s-e-u-m." Tell students that the word *museum* begins with the letter "m." Ask them to practice making the /m/ sound. Now direct students' attention to the sentence at the bottom of the page. Ask them if they recognize any words in the sentence. While pointing to the words, read the sentence. Ask students to read the sentence with you while you point to the words. Point out that the letter "u" is in this word two times. The first "u" is long and the second "u" is short. Practice the short /ŭ/ and the long /ū/ sounds.

Building Knowledge and Comprehension

Show students the card. Ask them to read the word *museum* at the top of the card as you point to it. Ask them to read the sentence at the bottom of the card as you point to each word. Discuss with students what a museum is and the different types of museums in your community. If possible, plan a trip to a local museum in your community. For example, if you are learning about dinosaurs, visit the closest museum that features dinosaurs. If a field trip is not possible, call your local museum and ask about programs they have to help serve the surrounding schools. Ask if a museum employee is available to come to your classroom and give a presentation. If an employee is unable to visit, the museum may have kits available for teachers to check out. You may also be able to take a virtual tour of a museum on the Internet. Search websites for museums before class and bookmark them to share with students.

Time to Differentiate!

For English language learners, help build vocabulary. Show students pictures of museums, both inside and out. Describe each picture and have students repeat key words.

For below-level students, preread the word and sentence on the card. Point to each word as you read it. Then ask students to read with you. Invite various students to point to the words while you read as a group.

museum

A **museum** is where you can learn about many things.

Activating Prior Knowledge

If possible, take students to the school library when discussing this card to help build their knowledge. Show students Social Studies Card 9. Ask them to look at the picture and describe what they see. Ask students where they think the picture was taken. Discuss with students why we have libraries. Tell them that a library is a place where people can go to check out books, but there are also other things we can do in a library. Ask students to share their experiences with going to a library. Discuss the other things a person can do at a library. For example, students do research for projects, read magazines or newspapers, use the Internet, and listen to stories. Discuss with students who works in the library and who you ask if you need help. If possible, arrange for a librarian from your local public library to come to your class and talk about how to get a library card.

Language Development

Show students the card again. Ask them to describe what they see in the picture. Tell students to look at the word at the top of the card. Ask them what they think the word is. Tell them to look at the letter the word begins with and the picture for a clue. Tell them the word is *library* and ask them to read it with you while you point to it. Tell students that the word *library* begins with the letter "l." Ask them to practice making the /l/ sound. Ask students to think of other words that begin with the letter "l" and list them on the board. Now direct students' attention to the sentence at the bottom of the page. Ask them if they recognize any words in the sentence. While pointing to the words, read the sentence. Ask students to read the sentence with you while you point to the words.

Building Knowledge and Comprehension

Show students the card. Ask them to read the word *library* at the top of the card as you point to it. Ask them to read the sentence at the bottom of the card as you point to each word. Take students on a tour of the library for this part of your discussion. Show students where the librarian's desk is and explain to them that the librarian is the person to ask if they need help with the library. Tell students about the Dewey Decimal System and the way the library is arranged. Be sure to show students where the books are that would be appropriate for them to check out. Model how to remove a book from the shelf and remember where to put it back. Have students make book markers to use in the library. Give each student a paint stick to keep in his or her desk to use as a book marker when attending the library. Give students time to decorate them with markers or paint. When they are finished decorating, spray the markers with varnish so the marker ink won't rub off on the books.

Time to Differentiate!

For English language learners, use a visit to the library to build vocabulary and background knowledge. Show students the various areas of the library, and label them with index cards. Then say each word again, and ask students to go and stand near the correct label.

For below-level students, preteach the letter "l." Write the letter on the board and have students trace it with their fingers. Name other words that begin with the letter "l" and have students repeat after you.

library

The **library** is where you find great books.

Unit 1
My Community

Introductory Lesson—Part A

Objective

Pre-K and K–2 Standard 6.5: Students relate stories to their lives and personal experiences.

Skills

- understanding the main idea of text
- applying the main idea to real-life situations
- recognizing the connection between text and real-life situations

Materials

- Social Studies Cards 1–9
- grocery list
- advertisements from a local grocery store

Word Study

- grocery store
- buy
- people
- fire station
- safe
- place
- neighborhood
- hospital
- school
- learn
- doctors
- nurses
- park
- play
- sorted
- post office
- mail
- museum
- library

Comprehension and Skills

Part 1: Lesson Length: approx. 20 minutes

1. Begin the lesson by reading a grocery list to students, but do not tell them it is a grocery list. After reading the items on the list, ask students to tell you what the list is. Ask if they have ever seen a list like this one. Ask, "Where would somebody take this list?" Point out that this is a grocery list and that people would use a list like this to buy food at a grocery store.

2. Divide the class into groups of three or four. Give each group an advertisement from a local grocery store to examine. Instruct students to look at the pictures and words in their advertisements to determine what someone could buy at the grocery store.

3. After the groups have had time to look at the advertisement, let each group share with the class what a person might buy at the grocery store featured in their ad. Encourage them to show pictures or words from the advertisement. Now send the groups back to their seats to make a grocery list of what the members of the group would buy at the grocery store. Be available to assist students in locating words from the advertisements to help create their lists.

4. Discuss with the class the importance of using what we read in our daily lives. Tell students that they were using nonfiction material and applying it to a real-life situation. Shuffle Social Studies Cards 1–9 so that they are out of order. Ask students to look for the place where they would go to buy the items on their grocery lists.

Unit 1
My Community

Introductory Lesson—Part A *(cont.)*

Comprehension and Skills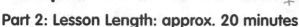

Part 2: Lesson Length: approx. 20 minutes

1. Explain to students that you are going to describe a place. Students should close their eyes and picture the description in their minds. Instruct students not to call out the answer, but to raise their hands. Give clues until a majority of students are raising their hands.

2. Describe a fire station using the following clues:

   - This is a building with a big garage door on it.
   - People live and work here.
   - The people who work here like to help others.
   - There are very big trucks here.
   - There is a big water hose here.
   - A siren goes off here.
   - The people who work here wear helmets.
   - The people who work here are brave.

3. Once most students have determined what you are talking about, ask them to open their eyes and share their ideas. Ask, "Did you guess a fire station?" Point out that you gave students information and they were able to picture in their minds the place that was being described. Students were using nonfiction information and applying it to something in real life. This skill is important for a reader.

4. Display Social Studies Card 1 for students.

5. Ask them to look closely at the picture. Allow time for students to get a good look and start thinking about what they are seeing. Explain that just by looking at the picture, they can gather much information. They can use this information to help them answer questions. Also, the picture can help them in case they ever go to the place in the picture. Explain how important it is to use what we learn in books and other materials in our lives.

6. Repeat this activity with any of the remaining cards in this unit (Social Studies Cards 2–9).

Assessment

Choose a Social Studies Card (1–9) at random. Have students look at the picture and analyze the location. Then ask them to explain how using this information can help them in their lives.

Have students explain how using an advertisement helped to create a grocery list. Have them explain how they were able to identify the Social Studies Card with the picture of a grocery store.

Unit 1
My Community

Focus Lesson

Objective

Pre-K and K–2 Standard 6.5: Students relate stories to their lives and personal experiences.

Skills

- understanding the main idea of text
- applying the main idea to real-life situations
- recognizing the connection between text and real-life situations

Materials

- Social Studies Cards 2 and 3
- chalk or whiteboard markers
- chalkboard or whiteboard
- crayons
- student copies of Activity 2 (page 58)
- writing paper
- envelopes
- student copies of Activity 3 (page 59)

Word Study

- park
- play
- sorted
- post office
- mail

Comprehension and Skills

Part 1: Lesson Length: approx. 20 minutes

1. Invite each student to share an experience that he or she has had at a park. Ask students, "Why are there parks? Why are they necessary? What do people do at parks?" Hold up Social Studies Card 2 and invite students to read the word at the top of the card. Ask them what sound the first letter makes. Then add the "-ark" to the /p/ sound, blending these sounds together to say "park." Now read the sentence at the bottom of the card.

2. Ask students what the word *play* means, and write their responses on the board. Have one student at a time act out something that can be done at the park. As students guess, make a list of these activities. After each student has had a turn, point out that the word *play* can mean many things. Hold up Social Studies Card 2 and ask students, "What are the children in the picture doing? Why do people go to parks?" Allow time for students to respond.

3. Distribute copies of Activity 2 (page 58) and read the directions at the top of the page. Above each sentence, students are to draw a picture of what they can do at a park. Have them do this activity at their seats or at a center. Read the sentences to students before they begin to work.

4. Finally, invite students to share their drawings, comparing and contrasting what they each drew. Discuss which of these activities they have done at a park.

Focus Lesson (cont.)

Comprehension and Skills

Part 2: Lesson Length: approx. 20 minutes

1. Hold up Social Studies Card 3 and have students explain what this place is and what goes on here. Have them sound out the first letter of the word *post*. Point to the word *post* and read it with the class. Now point to the next word and read *office*. Next have students read the sentence at the bottom of the card with you, pointing to each word as you read. Read the sentence twice to allow students a chance to read all of the words.

2. Ask students if they have ever been to a post office. Invite them to share what they saw there. Ask, "What did it look like? What were people doing there? Did the post office look like the one on Social Studies Card 3?"

3. Tell students that you would like to design a post office in the classroom. Ask them to help you make a list of things that will be needed to set it up. This list might include a post office box for each student, an outgoing mailbox, someone to sort the mail, and stamps. After planning the post office, make arrangements to set one up. Distribute paper to students and encourage them to write letters and draw pictures for each other. Students need to write the name of the student to whom they want to send the letter. Place all letters in the outgoing mailbox. Have two or three students sort through the mail and place letters in the correct boxes. Each day you can have a different group of students sort the mail and deliver it to the correct box.

Comprehension and Skills

Part 3: Lesson Length: approx. 20 minutes

1. Have students write a letter to a family member or to a friend. Students will probably need assistance in writing letters. Encourage students to draw pictures to illustrate their letters. With the assistance of an older student or an adult, have each student write the delivery and return addresses on an envelope. Then have each student put a stamp on the envelope to put in a mailbox. Encourage students to think about where the letter will be going before it reaches its destination. Have students explain how the post office sorts mail, comparing it to how they sort the mail in class. Ask them, "How are these two activities alike? How are they different?"

2. Distribute copies of Activity 3 (page 59). Have students circle the correct answer to each question.

Time to Differentiate!

For above-level students, encourage them to use more descriptive language in their letters.

Assessment

Ask students to explain what they learned about the post office by reading Social Studies Card 3. Ask, "How did reading the card help you understand more about the post office?"

Center Activities

Objective

Pre-K and K–2 Standard 6.5: Students relate stories to their lives and personal experiences.

Center #1:
Exploring the Hospital

Materials

- Social Studies Card 5
- student copies of Activity 5 (page 61)
- white paper for each student
- colored pencils or crayons

Comprehension and Skills

1. Distribute copies of Activity 5 (page 61) to each student. Read the directions at the top of the page while students read along. Explain and clarify the directions. Circulate around the room and ask students why they crossed out the items they did.

2. Show Social Studies Card 5 and have students read the card with you. Have them make the sounds for each of the letters in the word *hospital* and then sound it out. Read the sentence at the bottom of the card, pointing to each word as you read.

3. Have paper available for each student to draw a picture of a person who needs to go to a hospital or one who is already a patient. When finished, allow students to share their pictures. Ask students to tell how the hospital can help the person in their pictures. Look at Social Studies Card 5 and ask, "Which of the workers in this picture will help the patient in your pictures? How do you think the patient will feel while at the hospital? What does the patient need? Will the people at the hospital be able to help the people in your drawings?"

4. When all students have participated in this center, bind all of the drawings together to create a class book. Store this book in the class library, and read it on occasion to reinforce what students have learned about the hospital.

Center #2:
Fire Station Maze

Materials

- pencils
- student copies of Activity 1 (page 57)

Comprehension and Skills

1. Distribute copies of Activity 1 (page 57) to each student. Read the directions at the top of the page.

2. Discuss with students different tools that firefighters use.

3. Have students complete the activity page independently.

Center Activities *(cont.)*

Center #3:
Grocery Store Pictures

Materials

- Social Studies Card 4
- student copies of Activity 4 (page 60)
- white paper
- crayons or colored pencils

Comprehension and Skills

1. Hold up Social Studies Card 4. Encourage students to read the words at the top of the card and the sentence at the bottom of the card. Determine if they are able to read the words independently. Remind students to use pictures as context clues to help them decode words and their meanings.

2. Distribute copies of Activity 4 (page 60). Explain that this is a picture of an imaginary grocery store. Point out that there are three aisles in this particular grocery store. Have students locate aisle 1 and point to it. Then have students point to aisles 2 and 3. Now read the directions at the top of the page to students. Work together to sound out the words listed on this page. The first word on the page is *meat*. Meat can be found in aisle 3, so the number 3 should be written next to the word *meat*. Continue in this manner until all of the words have the correct aisle number written beside them.

3. Using crayons or colored pencils, have students color foods in this grocery store. Point out that there are a wide variety of items that can be found in the grocery store. There are many different foods available. Using the picture of the grocery store, have students locate the aisle where they would find apples. Then ask them to determine the aisle where they would find lobster. Now let volunteers name an item as their classmates find the correct aisle.

4. Give each student a sheet of paper to draw a picture of something he or she would like to buy at a grocery store. When all students have finished their pictures, staple them together to create a class book. On the cover, write "A Trip to the Grocery Store." Read the book to the class and store it in the class library.

Unit 1
My Community

Introductory Lesson—Part B

Objectives

Pre-K Standard 6.5: Students relate stories to their lives and personal experiences.

K–2 Standard 7.2: Students understand the main idea and supporting details of simple expository information.

Skills

- identifying proposition statements
- identifying support statements
- recognizing proposition and support in text

Materials

- Social Studies Cards 6–9
- chalk or whiteboard markers
- chalkboard or whiteboard
- white paper
- crayons, markers, or colored pencils

Word Study

- school
- learn
- library
- great
- neighborhood
- live
- work
- play
- museum

Comprehension and Skills

Part 1: Lesson Length: approx. 20 minutes

1. Display Social Studies Card 7. Read the word *neighborhood* together while reviewing the beginning and ending sounds of this word. Call on volunteers to describe things that are in the area near their homes. After students have shared, draw some of these things on the board. When finished, draw a big circle around all of these objects. Explain that this area is called a neighborhood. A neighborhood is what immediately surrounds your home. Discuss what students like about their neighborhoods.

2. Distribute the white paper and demonstrate how to fold it to look like a brochure (folded vertically into thirds). Have students draw pictures of things that they like to do in and around their neighborhoods. Encourage them to draw the people and interesting features of their neighborhoods.

3. When students are finished, discuss and identify the reasons students gave for why they like their neighborhoods. Explain that the reasons they shared support their beliefs that they have a good neighborhood. We can find these same types of supportive statements in what we read.

Introductory Lesson—Part B *(cont.)*

Comprehension and Skills

Part 2: Lesson Length: approx. 20 minutes

1. Display Social Studies Card 6 and ask students to read the word at the top of the card. Have them make the sound of the first letter in the word. Now read the rest of the word and have students repeat the word. Have them take turns using *school* in a sentence. Ask them to read the sentences at the bottom of the card. Tell students that both sentences have the word *school* in them and have them raise their hands when they see or hear the word *school*.

2. Ask students whether they think that school is important, and invite them to share their opinions. Ask, "How can you convince others that school is important?" While students individually share their ideas, make notes on the board of key words and phrases that they are using to support their ideas. When finished, explain that you found the *proposition* and the *support* for school in the words that students were using.

3. Ask students to explain how they feel about learning to read, and then have them support their ideas with at least three good reasons. Point out the proposition and support in their responses.

Comprehension and Skills

Part 3: Lesson Length: approx. 20 minutes

1. Lead a discussion about places to visit in their community. Hold up Social Studies Cards 8 and 9 and ask students to sound out the words at the top of the cards.

2. Ask students if they have ever been to a library or a museum. Point out the location of the library in the classroom and in the school. Find out if students know where the nearest public library and museum are located. Ask, "What makes libraries different? Why do people go to the museum?"

3. Ask students to explain why people should visit a library or museum. Model examples of supportive statements: "You should go to the airplane museum because you can learn a lot about airplanes." Point out that when we read, the author is often trying to convince us to do or believe something.

4. Distribute plain white paper and ask students to draw a sign inviting people to the public library or museum. Display Social Studies Cards 8 and 9 so that they may refer to them. Students should color their signs.

Assessment

Hold up Social Studies Card 7 and have students list three reasons supporting the idea that they live in a good neighborhood. Look for statements of support in their responses.

Center Activities

Objectives

Pre-K Standard 6.5: Students relate stories to their lives and personal experiences.

K–2 Standard 7.2: Students understand the main idea and supporting details of simple expository information.

Center #1: Classroom Museum

Materials

- student copies of Activity 8 (page 64)
- chalk or whiteboard markers
- chalkboard or whiteboard
- crayons, markers, or colored pencils
- white construction paper
- decorating materials for posters

Comprehension and Skills

1. Distribute copies of Activity 8 (page 64) to students. Read the directions at the top of the page. Tell students that they need to circle the reasons why they would go to a museum. Tell them not to circle the reasons that do not fit. Read each reason aloud and allow time for students to circle them. When finished, have them color the pictures on this page. Ask students, "Which of these pictures shows a museum that you would like to visit?"

2. As a class, have students brainstorm ideas for a museum that could be put together in the classroom. Discuss what ideas would work the best and would be of most interest to them. Set up a plan and a schedule for creating this museum. Involve students as much as possible in constructing this museum. To generate a name for the museum, have a contest with students or brainstorm as a class for the best name.

3. Once the museum has been established and all students have gone through it, give each student a large sheet of white construction paper at a center. Instruct them to design a poster to post throughout the school to encourage other students to visit the museum. Brainstorm reasons to support visiting the museum. To assist students in spelling and writing, write on the board some agreed-upon phrases that can be used to support and validate a trip to the classroom museum.

4. Have students decorate the posters with pictures and other materials at the center. Hang the posters throughout the school to generate interest. Schedule times for other classes to come and visit your museum. Discuss with students how their supportive statements were able to interest others to visit the classroom. Explain the importance of being able to make propositions and then backing them up with supportive statements.

Center Activities *(cont.)*

Center #2:
Building a Neighborhood

Materials

- Social Studies Card 7
- student copies of Activity 7 (page 63)
- crayons, colored pencils, or markers
- blocks or building materials

Comprehension and Skills

1. Hold up Social Studies Card 7 and ask students to read the word on the top of the card. Then read the sentence at the bottom of the card, pointing to each word as you read. Read the sentence again, and encourage students to read along with you this time. Ask them to review with you what the picture is about.

2. Distribute copies of Activity 7 (page 63). While students look at the page, explain that this is a map of an imaginary neighborhood and that they are to answer the questions on the page. (You will probably need to arrange this activity for when you are available to help with spelling and wording, as this activity may be too difficult for students to do independently.)

3. Have students color the neighborhood. If time allows, you may choose to ask further questions that they can answer using the neighborhood map. Here are some suggestions:

   - Who do you think walks to school?
   - What types of activities can kids do at Panther Park?
   - What street is the library on?
   - Which is closer to the library, the park or the school?

4. At the center, provide blocks or other building materials for students to build models of their neighborhoods. Have them take into consideration the number of houses, trees, businesses, parks, cars, and so forth. Allow time for students to share their models with a partner or in small groups.

Unit 1
My Community

Wrap-up

Introduction

The wrap-up activities tie together the skills that have been taught throughout the unit. They provide opportunities for students to show the skills they have learned within this unit.

Objectives

Pre-K and K–2 Standard 6.5: Students relate stories to their lives and personal experiences.

K–2 Standard 7.2: Students understand the main idea and supporting details of simple expository information.

Materials

- chalk or whiteboard markers
- chalkboard or whiteboard
- Social Studies Cards 1–9
- large piece of butcher paper
- crayons, markers, or colored pencils
- rulers
- student copies of page 55
- pencils

Comprehension and Skills

1. Explain to students that they will be making a mural of their community. Brainstorm a list of places found in a community. Divide the class into nine groups. Give each group a card from Social Studies Cards 1–9. The group members are to look over their card to determine what this place is in the community. Students are to think about why this place is in the community, where it is located, and how it should be represented on the mural. Have students imagine what this place looks like in their real-life community and try to base their picture on that place.

2. Prior to having students work on the community mural, you may wish to use a ruler to draw streets and corners on the mural so that the community is somewhat organized and it is easy to locate places.

3. Invite groups who are finished planning to work on the mural. Students will need to draw the locations in pencil and then color them. An adult should be on hand to assist with writing and spelling, if needed. Remind students to make their places in the community look similar to those in real life so that others will be able to recognize them. They can include symbols or signs that would be helpful.

4. Distribute copies of page 55 and have each student make a poster to serve as an advertisement for the place that he or she drew on the mural.

Community Mural

Think about the place you drew on the community mural. Make a poster for that place. Make people want to visit.

Come see the . . .

Notes

Help the firefighter get to the **fire station**. Look for the things you would find in a **fire station**. They will help you get through the maze.

Draw a picture to go with each thing you can do at the **park**. Circle the things you like to do at the **park**.

Have a picnic.

Fly a kite.

Ride a bike.

Walk a dog.

Name _____

Unit 1
My Community

What can you do at the **post office**? Circle the answer to each question.

Can you . . .

mail a letter?
yes   no

buy stamps?
yes   no

buy a fish?
yes   no

see a movie?
yes   no

Look at the **grocery store** map. Write the number of the aisle where you can get the following foods.

meat _____   bread _____   milk _____

corn _____   fish _____   grapes _____

Cross out the things that don't belong at a **hospital**. Color the rest of the picture.

Unit 1
My Community

Name _____

Here are some places you can find in a **school**. Draw a line from each label to the place on the drawing that it names.

library   classroom   cafeteria

auditorium   computer center

Look at this **neighborhood** map. Then answer the questions.

Who lives next to the library?

_____

....

_____

What street is the fire station on?

_____

....

_____

Who lives closest to the school?

_____

....

_____

What street does Lin live on?

_____

....

_____

Unit 1
My Community

Why might you go to a **museum**? Circle each reason.

to find out about dinosaurs

to buy shoes

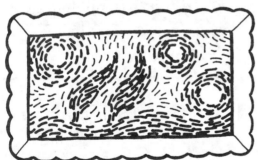

to look at paintings

to learn about life in the past

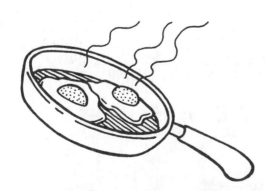

to learn how to cook

to learn about science

Put a check in front of each rule you
should follow at the **library**.

☐ Talk quietly.

☐ Run in the hall.

☐ Ask for help if you can't find what you need.

☐ Use your library card to check out books.

☐ Eat food in the library.

☐ Return library books when they are due.

Can you add another rule?

_____

_____

My Community

Community Workers

Kinds of Land and Water

The United States

Introduction to Unit 2: Community Workers

Community Workers is a perfect theme to teach after students learn about their community. Students will be excited to draw connections between the nonfiction text passages and their own personal experiences. Important vocabulary terms such as *teacher*, *firefighter*, *police*, *safe*, and *crossing guard* are introduced. In this unit, students will learn to recognize the importance of identifying the main idea and important facts in text.

Skills Taught in This Unit

- identifying the main idea by looking at pictures
- locating the main idea in text
- understanding the main idea
- locating important facts in text
- recognizing important facts and less important facts
- identifying the important facts by looking at pictures
- explaining important facts in their own words

Directions for the Teacher

You have many different options when teaching this unit. You can use the nonfiction text pages (Social Studies Cards) and teach the content using the strategies that precede each text passage. Or, you can teach nonfiction skills and strategies by teaching the whole unit, starting with the introductory lesson, then teaching the focus lesson, and then following up with the center activities. This format repeats for the second lesson in the unit. Conclude the unit by teaching the wrap-up activity to tie all the nonfiction text and skills together.

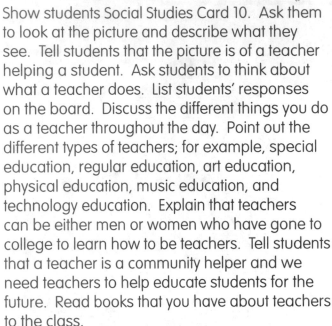
Activating Prior Knowledge

Show students Social Studies Card 10. Ask them to look at the picture and describe what they see. Tell students that the picture is of a teacher helping a student. Ask students to think about what a teacher does. List students' responses on the board. Discuss the different things you do as a teacher throughout the day. Point out the different types of teachers; for example, special education, regular education, art education, physical education, music education, and technology education. Explain that teachers can be either men or women who have gone to college to learn how to be teachers. Tell students that a teacher is a community helper and we need teachers to help educate students for the future. Read books that you have about teachers to the class.

Language Development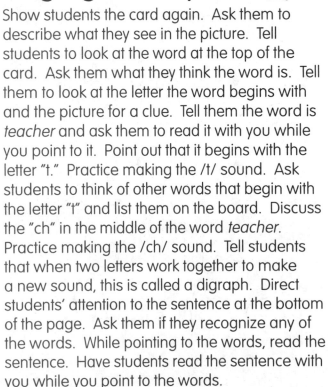

Show students the card again. Ask them to describe what they see in the picture. Tell students to look at the word at the top of the card. Ask them what they think the word is. Tell them to look at the letter the word begins with and the picture for a clue. Tell them the word is *teacher* and ask them to read it with you while you point to it. Point out that it begins with the letter "t." Practice making the /t/ sound. Ask students to think of other words that begin with the letter "t" and list them on the board. Discuss the "ch" in the middle of the word *teacher*. Practice making the /ch/ sound. Tell students that when two letters work together to make a new sound, this is called a digraph. Direct students' attention to the sentence at the bottom of the page. Ask them if they recognize any of the words. While pointing to the words, read the sentence. Have students read the sentence with you while you point to the words.

Building Knowledge and Comprehension

Show students the card. Ask them to read the word *teacher* at the top of the card as you point to it. Read the sentence at the bottom of the card. Ask students to read the sentence at the bottom of the card again as you point to each word. Discuss with students how someone can become a teacher. Explain to students that you need to go to college and study hard to become a teacher. Talk about how there are different types of teachers. Make a list of students' ideas about different types of teachers on the board or on chart paper. Create a school center for students to visit. Provide desks for the students and other materials such as pointers, a dry erase board and markers, big books, book stands, etc. Model for students how to play school in the center. Ask several students to participate in the pretend classroom in front of the rest of the students.

Time to Differentiate!

For English language learners, preteach the vocabulary needed for the Building Knowledge and Comprehension lesson. Show students a pointer, big book, book stand, etc. Say each word as you show the item, and then ask students to repeat it.

For below-level students, preteach the /ch/ sound. Say other words that have the /ch/ sound and have students repeat them. Write those words on the board and have students underline the "ch" digraph.

teacher

Artist Corner

The **teacher** helps us learn new things.

Activating Prior Knowledge

Show students Social Studies Card 11. Ask them to look at the card closely and describe what they see. Ask them to tell you what they see in the picture, who this person is, and where they think the picture was taken. If possible, arrange for a firefighter to come and visit your school the same day you discuss this card. Ask students if any of their parents are firefighters or if they know a firefighter. Ask them to share any experiences they may have had visiting a fire station. Ask students to brainstorm all of the things that a firefighter does. Have students draw pictures of firefighters in action. Read books that you have in class about firefighters.

Language Development

Show students the card and ask them again to describe what they see in the picture. Tell them that the word at the top of the card says *firefighter*. Ask them to look at the first part of the word *fire*. Ask them to tell you what the word *fire* begins with. After they respond that the word *fire* begins with the letter "f," ask them to practice making the /f/ sound. Do the same with the word *fighter*. Explain to students that *firefighter* is a compound word. Direct students' attention to the sentence at the bottom of the card. Tell them to look carefully and see if they recognize any words in the sentence. While pointing to the words, read the sentence to students. Ask students to read the sentence with you several times while you point to the words. Students can take turns pointing to the words while the remainder of the class reads the sentence out loud.

Building Knowledge and Comprehension

Show students the card again. Ask them to read the word *firefighter* at the top of the card as you point to it. Ask them to read the sentence at the bottom of the card as you point to it. Write the "Five Little Firefighters" poem (see below) on a sheet of chart paper. Read the poem several times while pointing to the words. Have students take turns pointing to the words with a pointer while the rest of the class reads. After students read the poem, have them take turns acting it out.

Five Little Firefighters

Five little firefighters sleeping in a row

Ding goes the bell, down the pole one goes.

Four little firefighters sleeping in a row

Ding goes the bell, down another one goes.
(continue until none are left)

Time to Differentiate!

For English language learners, preteach the poem for the Building Knowledge and Comprehension lesson. Echo-read the poem several times with students. Then say each line with gestures or movements to help students understand the words.

For below-level students, scaffold the discussion activities by encouraging them to talk with partners before sharing their thoughts or experiences with the class. If needed, model for them how to answer in complete sentences.

firefighter

The **firefighter** has an important job.

Activating Prior Knowledge

Show students Social Studies Card 12. Ask them to look at the card and describe what they see. Tell students that the picture is of a police officer talking with a little girl. Ask students what the two people might be talking about. Tell students that police officers are here to help the public and the little girl may be asking the police officer for help. Discuss other reasons why we need police officers. For example, we need them for security, to direct traffic, and to educate the public. Ask students to share any experiences they have had with police officers. If possible, ask a police officer to visit your classroom. Read books that you may have about police officers to students. Ask students to draw pictures of police officers in action and label their pictures.

Language Development

Ask students to look at the card. Ask them to describe what they see. Direct their attention to the word *police* at the top of the card. Tell them the word is *police* and ask them if they can tell you what it begins with. After they respond, ask them to practice making the /p/ sound. Tell students you are going to say the word *police* and you want them to listen closely and then tell you what sound they hear at the end of the word. After they tell you that they hear the /s/ sound at the end of the word *police*, explain to them that the /s/ sound is actually made with a "c." Explain that the "c" in this case is making the soft "c" sound /s/ and the "e" at the end of the word is silent. Direct students' attention to the sentence at the bottom of the card. Ask them if they recognize any words in the sentence. Point to the words and read the sentence out loud. Ask students to read the sentence with you. While reading the sentence, have students snap their fingers when they hear the word *police*.

Building Knowledge and Comprehension

Show students the card. Ask them to read the word *police* at the top of the card as you point to it. Ask them to read the sentence at the bottom of the card as you point to each word. Talk about the different jobs a police officer does. Also discuss the different ways that police officers travel. For example, some police officers ride on horses and others drive cars. Police officers also travel by bicycle, van, and motorcycle. Discuss with students how all police officers are there to help people. Tell students that whenever they feel afraid, they can find a police officer to help them.

Time to Differentiate!

For English language learners, help them build background knowledge by introducing key words and concepts. Explain and act out directing traffic, giving directions, and talking on a radio. Then repeat the words and concepts and ask students to act them out with you.

For below-level students, preteach the soft "c" sound /s/. Say the word *police*, emphasizing the /s/ sound at the end of the word. Write the word on the board and circle the "ce" pattern. Repeat this with additional words such as *rice*, *face*, *place*, and *juice*.

police

The **police** help make our neighborhoods safe.

Activating Prior Knowledge

Show students Social Studies Card 13. Ask students to look at the card closely and describe in detail what they see. Tell students that this is a picture of a crossing guard. Ask them to think about what a crossing guard does. Tell them that crossing guards are there to help people cross the street. Ask them where a person might see a crossing guard. Discuss how a crossing guard often helps students cross the street to get to school, but that a crossing guard is sometimes necessary at other busy intersections. Discuss with students that a crossing guard's job is to keep students and adults safe, so it is important to obey crossing guards. Discuss with students the crossing guards near your school (if you have them). Ask them if the crossing guard uses a sign or a flag that has any words on it. If possible, invite the local crossing guard to come and speak to the class.

Language Development

Show the card to the students. Ask them to describe what they see. Ask them to look closely at the two words at the top of the card. Tell them the phrase is *crossing guard* and you would like them to look at the first word. Ask them what letters the first word begins with. After students respond, have them practice making the /cr/ blend. Ask them what letter the word *guard* begins with. After they respond, have them practice making the /g/ sound. Ask students to look at the word *crossing* again. Point out that the word ends in "-ing," and have them practice making that sound. Direct students' attention to the sentence at the bottom of the card. Ask them if they recognize any words in the sentence. While pointing to the words, read the sentence. Ask students to read the sentence with you while you point to the words.

Building Knowledge and Comprehension

Show students the card. Ask them to read the words *crossing guard* at the top of the card as you point to them. Ask them to read the sentence at the bottom of the card as you point to each word. Discuss with students again how crossing guards are there to help people and how important it is for all people to obey them. Borrow the sign or flag (or make your own stop sign) that is used by crossing guards at your school. If the flag or sign has the word *stop* on it, ask students to practice reading it. Remind students that there are stop signs on streets and discuss the importance of cars obeying the stop signs. Take students out to see the playground and discuss safety while walking to school. Draw or tape off a crosswalk area. Pretend you are a crossing guard and have them practice crossing the "street" while obeying the crossing guard. Discuss with students how important it is to listen very carefully to the guard and do exactly as they are told.

Time to Differentiate!

For English language learners, build students' background knowledge prior to the lessons. Show students the card. Point to various things in the picture and name them. Ask students to repeat the words. Write those words on sticky notes and place them on the picture.

For below-level students, preview the card in a small group. Read the words at the top of the card and ask students to repeat them. While pointing to each word, read the sentence at the bottom of the card. Repeat this several times.

crossing guard

Let the **crossing guard** help you.

sanitation worker

Activating Prior Knowledge

Show students Social Studies Card 14. Ask them to look at the card and describe what they see. Ask students to think about what a sanitation worker does. Tell students that sanitation workers are sometimes called garbage collectors. Discuss why it is so important that we have sanitation workers. Talk about what would happen if nobody came to pick up the trash. Try to go outside to observe when the garbage truck comes to pick up your school trash. Ask students what the garbage cans look like at their homes compared to the garbage bins at school. Read any books that you may have about sanitation workers to students. Ask students to draw a picture of a sanitation worker and label the picture. If a parent of a student is a sanitation worker, invite that parent to come and talk to the class.

Language Development

Share the card with students. Ask them to describe what they see. Ask them to look at the two words at the top of the card. Tell them the phrase is *sanitation worker*. Ask them what letter the first word begins with. After students respond, have them practice making the /s/ sound. Ask students what letter the word *worker* begins with. After they respond, have them practice making the /w/ sound. Ask students to look at the word *worker* again. Write the word *worker* on the board, separating the word *work* from the "-er" ending. Tell students that the word *work* is the root word and the "-er" is an ending. Tell them that you are going to change the word by changing the ending. Add new endings to the word such as the following: "-s," "-ed," and "-ing." Explain that changing the ending of the word changes the meaning of the word. Discuss the meaning of each new word.

Building Knowledge and Comprehension

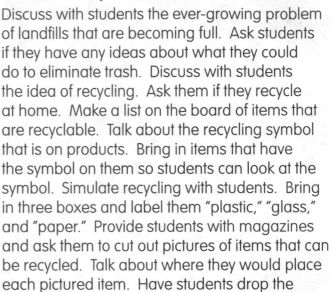

Discuss with students the ever-growing problem of landfills that are becoming full. Ask students if they have any ideas about what they could do to eliminate trash. Discuss with students the idea of recycling. Ask them if they recycle at home. Make a list on the board of items that are recyclable. Talk about the recycling symbol that is on products. Bring in items that have the symbol on them so students can look at the symbol. Simulate recycling with students. Bring in three boxes and label them "plastic," "glass," and "paper." Provide students with magazines and ask them to cut out pictures of items that can be recycled. Talk about where they would place each pictured item. Have students drop the pictures into the correct boxes.

Time to Differentiate!

For English language learners, scaffold the recycling activity in the Building Knowledge and Comprehension lesson. Show students the magazine pictures, and have them labeled in English. Say each word and have students repeat it. Let students talk with partners about which of the three groups it belongs to.

For below-level students, scaffold the recycling activity in the Building Knowledge and Comprehension lesson. Show students several magazine pictures. Explain what each one is made of, and then decide as a group which box it belongs in. Then distribute one magazine picture to each pair of students and have them place the picture in the correct box.

sanitation worker

The **sanitation worker** keeps our town clean.

Unit 2
Community Workers

nurse

Activating Prior Knowledge

Ask students to look at Social Studies Card 15. Ask students to describe what they see in the picture. Tell students that the picture is of a nurse listening to a little girl's heart. Discuss what a nurse does. Explain that a nurse is a community helper and nursing is a profession that helps people. Ask students to talk about when they have seen a nurse. Ask if anyone has a nurse in his or her family. Point out that although nurses work at hospitals and doctor's offices, they work in other places too. On the board, make a list of the other places nurses work such as nursing homes, schools, sporting events, health clubs, and businesses. Remind students that when they visit the doctor, they usually see the nurse first. Talk about why it is important for nurses to help doctors and what information they find out about the patient for the doctor. If possible, arrange for the school nurse to speak to your class.

Language Development

Show students the card again. Ask them to describe what they see in the picture. Tell students to look at the word at the top of the card. Tell them the word is *nurse* and ask them to read it with you while you point to it. Read it several times. Segment the word *nurse*, "n-ur-se," and ask students to repeat after you. Tell students that the word *nurse* begins with the letter "n." Practice making the /n/ sound. Ask students what sound is at the end of the word. Point out that although the ending sound is /s/, it actually ends with the letter "e." Discuss the fact that the "e" is silent. Now direct students' attention to the sentence at the bottom of the page. While pointing to the words, read the sentence. Ask students to read the sentence with you while you point to the words.

Building Knowledge and Comprehension

Show students the card. Ask them to read the word *nurse* at the top of the card as you point to it. Ask them to read the sentence at the bottom of the card as you point to each word. Discuss with students the nurse's uniform. Explain to students what nurses used to wear and what they wear now. Talk about the fact that nurses used to wear hats. If possible, have examples (in books or photographs) of nurse uniforms, past and present, to show students. Tell students that both men and women can be nurses. Put uniforms in a drama center for students to try on and pretend to be a nurse. Read books about nurses to the class. Have each student write a page in a class book with the sentence frame, "Nurses help people by _____." Have students draw a picture to go with their sentences. Bind the pages together in a class book.

Time to Differentiate!

For English language learners, help them complete their sentences in the Building Knowledge and Comprehension lesson. Have students draw a picture of a nurse helping people. Then label their pictures in English. Then encourage each student to use the label to complete his or her sentence.

For below-level students, practice identifying the beginning and ending sounds of the word *nurse*. If needed, tell students what each sound is and have them repeat the sound after you. Name other words that begin with the letter "n," and have students repeat the words, emphasizing the /n/ sound at the beginning.

nurse

A **nurse** can help you when you are sick.

Activating Prior Knowledge

Show students Social Studies Card 16. Ask them to describe what they see. Ask students what is happening in the picture and where it was taken. Tell students the picture is of a dentist. Talk with students about how dentists can be both men and women. Ask students to share their experiences of going to the dentist. Explain how a dentist is a doctor who works to keep our mouths and teeth healthy. Talk about how a person must go to school for a very long time to become a dentist. Discuss what it is like at a typical dental appointment. Explain to students that a dental hygienist helps the dentist by looking at your teeth first. Talk about how the dental hygienist sometimes takes x-rays and cleans your teeth too. Read any books you may have about dentists to your class. Invite a dentist to come and talk to the class.

Language Development

Ask students to look at the card. Ask them to describe what they see. Direct their attention to the word *dentist* at the top of the card. Tell them the word is *dentist* and ask them if they can tell you what it begins with. After they respond, ask them to practice making the /d/ sound. Ask them what sound they hear at the end of the word. After they respond, ask them to practice making the /t/ sound. Ask students to practice making the sound of each letter in the word *dentist*. Point to each individual letter in the word and ask students to say its name and to make the sound it makes. Direct students' attention to the sentence at the bottom of the card. Ask them if they recognize any words in the sentence. While pointing to the words, read the sentence. Ask students to read the sentence with you while you point to the words.

Building Knowledge and Comprehension

Show students the card. Ask them to read the word *dentist* at the top of the card as you point to it. Ask them to read the sentence at the bottom of the card as you point to each word. Discuss with students the importance of taking care of teeth. Ask each student to count his or her teeth. Discuss why some students may have more teeth than others. Maybe some students have a set of molars that the others don't have yet. Talk to students about what types of foods are not good for their teeth, such as candy and sweets. Explain that some students will lose their teeth during the year. Talk with students about the importance of brushing and flossing their teeth. Make a poster to keep track each time a student loses a tooth throughout the school year.

Time to Differentiate!

For English language learners, preteach key vocabulary and concepts for the Building Knowledge and Comprehension lesson. Review the numbers 1–20. Show students where their molars are located. Act out brushing and flossing.

For below-level students, review the numbers 1–20 in preparation for the Building Knowledge and Comprehension lesson.

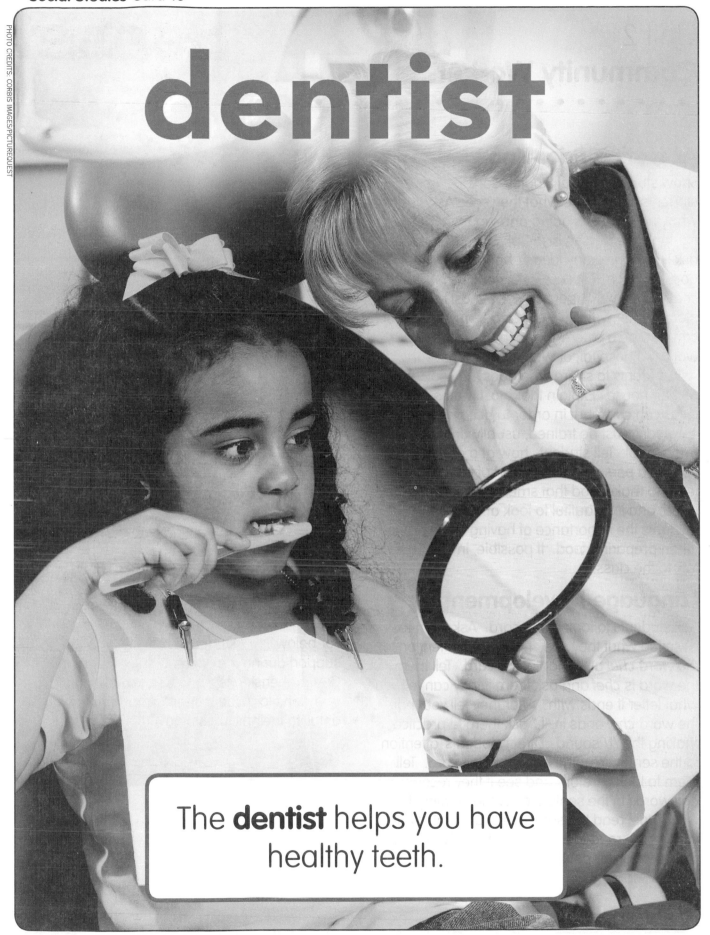

dentist

The **dentist** helps you have healthy teeth.

Introductory Lesson—Part A

Objectives

Pre-K Standard 5.13: Students use visual and verbal cues, including pictures, to comprehend new words and stories.

K–2 Standard 6.4: Students know the main ideas or themes of a story.

Skills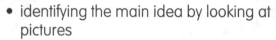

- identifying the main idea by looking at pictures
- locating the main idea in text
- understanding the main idea

Materials

- Social Studies Cards 10–13
- pictures from a magazine
- index cards printed with words that correspond to the magazine pictures
- short newspaper article of interest to students
- chalk or whiteboard markers
- chalkboard or whiteboard

Word Study

- teacher
- learn
- firefighter
- important
- police
- neighborhood
- safe
- crossing guard

Comprehension and Skills

Part 1: Lesson Length: approx. 20 minutes

1. Cut out pictures from a magazine and post them on the board. Mix up the index cards with the corresponding words, and post them on the other side of the board. As a class, see if students can match the words with the pictures.

2. Once all of the pictures and words have been matched, discuss how the words are the main ideas of the pictures. The pictures help students understand the words that they are reading. Explain that pictures will help them read. Reading requires us to look at pictures to help determine the words and main ideas. Reinforce the idea that illustrations help us understand the main points of what we are reading.

3. Hold up Social Studies Cards 10–13. As you hold up the pictures, have students determine the main idea of each card. (You may also choose to do this activity with cards used in other lessons.) Again, remind students to use the pictures to help them determine the main idea. Have students look at the card and speculate on what this picture is about and what the words might be saying. Allow students to share what the picture reminds them of. Ask, "Who is this person? What is he doing? Who is the lady? What is she doing? What do you think the words say? What is the point of this card?" Tell students to use the words to help them figure out the main idea.

Introductory Lesson—Part A (cont.)

Comprehension and Skills
Part 2: Lesson Length: approx. 20 minutes

1. Discuss the importance of being able to understand the main idea of what we read. Write the following question on the board: "What is the main idea?" Explain that not all the information in an article or story will help answer this question. Some information is more important.

2. Explain to students that you are going to read a newspaper article. Their job is to help you find the important information.

3. Read the title of the article to students. Show them any photos that accompany the article. Ask students if they can predict, or guess, what the article might be about. Write students' predictions on the board. Tell students that as they listen to the article, they are to raise their hands when they hear important information that will help them answer the question on the board.

4. Read the newspaper article to students.

5. After reading the article, ask students questions about the text. Create *Who, What, When, Where, Why,* and *How* questions. Write students' answers on the board. Help students check their answers against their predictions.

6. After discussing the article, ask students, "What is the main idea of this article? What is the article trying to tell us?" Using their answers, write a summary statement of the main idea on the board.

Comprehension and Skills
Part 3: Lesson Length: approx. 20 minutes

1. Distribute Social Studies Cards 10–13 to small groups. Have students look over the cards and discuss where they can locate the main idea of each card. The main idea might be in a word at the top of the card or in the sentences at the bottom.

2. For example, hold up Social Studies Card 13. Read the word *crossing* together as a class while reviewing the sounds of each letter. Then read the word *guard* together. Read the sentence together as a class. Now focus on each word in *crossing guard*, one at a time. Have students ask questions to help figure out the meaning of the word. Explain that good questions ask specific things about what we read. Discuss the meanings of the words and how asking questions helped them get to the answers. Reinforce the concept that asking good questions can help them understand the main idea.

Assessment

Instruct students to express in their own words how pictures and words can help us understand the main idea of what we read.

Give students a book and ask them to discuss what they think the main idea is, based on the pictures and sounding out any words they can read.

Unit 2
Community Workers

Focus Lesson

Objectives

Pre-K Standard 5.13: Students use visual and verbal cues, including pictures, to comprehend new words and stories.

K–2 Standard 6.4: Students know the main ideas or themes of a story.

Skills

- identifying the main idea by looking at pictures
- locating the main idea in text
- understanding the main idea

Materials

- Social Studies Cards 10–13
- chalk or whiteboard markers
- chalkboard or whiteboard

Word Study

- firefighter
- important
- teacher
- learn
- crossing guard
- help
- police
- safe

Comprehension and Skills

Part 1: Lesson Length: approx. 15 minutes

1. Begin this lesson by discussing the main idea. Hold up Social Studies Cards 10 and 11. For each card, have students identify the main idea. Point out how much information the class was able to determine from the two pictures.

2. Focusing on Social Studies Card 11, read the word at the top of the card with the class. Students should be able to tell you the beginning and ending sounds of the word *firefighter*. Sound out *firefighter* as you point to the word. Now read the sentence at the bottom of the card, pointing to each word as you read. Encourage students to define *firefighter* in their own words.

3. Have one student at a time act out what a firefighter does in his or her job. Let the other students guess what is being acted out. (Some ideas might include spraying water from a hose, riding in a truck, using an ax, or rescuing people.)

Focus Lesson (cont.)

Comprehension and Skills

Part 2: Lesson Length: approx. 15 minutes

1. Show students Social Studies Card 10. Ask students to share what they know about teachers. Ask them to create a sentence about teachers. Record students' sentences on the board. Read each sentence and point out the punctuation used at the end and the capital letter used at the beginning of each sentence. Now write the following questions on the board, one at a time:

   • Who can be a teacher?

   • Why do people want to be teachers?

   • What qualities make a good teacher?

2. Each time you write a question on the board, ask students to answer the question. Record their responses next to the appropriate question. As a class, identify the student responses that best answer each question.

3. Once you have identified student responses for each question, point out that students were able to organize information and identify the main idea. Students need to learn that not all information is needed to locate the main idea.

Comprehension and Skills

Part 3: Lesson Length: approx. 20 minutes

1. Discuss the definition of *crossing guard*. Write this term on the board. Encourage students to share their ideas.

2. Write the word *police* on the board and have students brainstorm what they know about police. If they have had experiences with police officers, they may wish to share them.

3. Hold up Social Studies Cards 12 and 13. By looking at the pictures, students should be able to determine the difference between a police officer and a crossing guard. Record students' observations on the board. Point out how the pictures helped students understand the main ideas.

4. Encourage students to read the sentences at the bottom of the cards with you. Point out the period at the end of the sentence and the capital letter at the beginning of the sentence.

Time to Differentiate!

For above-level students, ask students to write about what makes a good teacher, firefighter, crossing guard, or police officer. Remind students to state the main idea in the first sentence.

Assessment

Have students explain how to identify the main idea of a text. Using Social Studies Card 12, ask them to explain how this information is helpful in understanding more about the police. Then have them give examples of information that would not be helpful in learning about the police.

Unit 2
Community Workers

Center Activities

Objectives

Pre-K Standard 5.13: Students use visual and verbal cues, including pictures, to comprehend new words and stories.

K–2 Standard 6.4: Students know the main ideas or themes of a story.

Center #1:
Good Teachers

Materials

- Social Studies Card 10
- student copies of Activity 10 (page 98)
- colored pencils, markers, or crayons
- writing paper for each student

Comprehension and Skills

1. Hold up Social Studies Card 10 and ask students to look at the picture of the teacher. Read the word *teacher* at the top of the card. Review the definition of a teacher by reading the sentence at the bottom of the page, pointing to each word as you read.

2. Distribute copies of Activity 10 (page 98) to students. Point out that this page has a list of things that a teacher needs to do. Tell students to read the directions at the top of this page with you. Instruct them to point to each word as they read. Encourage them to find the word *teacher* in the sentence.

3. Have students go through the list of jobs that a teacher does and put a check mark next to the appropriate jobs. Discuss each of the jobs.

4. At the center, have students write a letter to their teacher. They should include what they like about their teacher and how he or she helps children learn. Be sure to have students decorate the letters with illustrations and borders. Allow time for them to share their work with other class members. You may choose to put these up on a bulletin board titled "Dear Teacher."

Center Activities (cont.)

Center #2: Police Officers and Firefighters

Materials

- Social Studies Card 11–12
- student copies of Activities 11 and 12 (pages 99 and 100)
- white paper for each student
- crayons, colored pencils, or markers

Comprehension and Skills

1. Hold up Social Studies Card 12. Discuss how the police officer might help the girl stay safe. Emphasize how pictures help us understand what we read. Sound out the word *police* and read the sentence.

2. Hold up Social Studies Card 11. Point to each word and read the sentence at the bottom of the card. Ask students to explain if this information is helpful in determining what the card is about.

3. Distribute copies of Activity 12 (page 100). Ask, "Which of these pictures shows the way that police officers get around the neighborhood?" (You may want to point out that some police officers ride in cars, on bikes, on motorcycles, and even on horses.)

4. Distribute copies of Activity 11 (page 99). Help students read the sentence at the top of the page. Then have students color the clothing that a firefighter would wear.

5. At the center, have students draw a picture showing the way police officers and firefighters help keep neighborhoods safe.

Center #3: Crossing Guards

Materials

- Social Studies Card 13
- student copies of Activity 13 (page 101)
- crayons, colored pencils, or markers
- pencils

Comprehension and Skills

1. Hold up Social Studies Card 13 and read the phrase *crossing guard* with students. Then read the sentence at the bottom of the page, encouraging students to read along with you. Ask them to locate certain words from the sentence. Continue until all the words in the sentence have been found.

2. Ask, "Why are crossing guards found near schools? Where else do you think a crossing guard would be helpful?" Have students support their answers.

3. At a center, distribute copies of Activity 13 (page 101). Read the directions at the top of the page and encourage students to follow along with you as you read. Ask them if they know where a crossing guard is near their school. Have students write what they think the crossing guard is saying on this page. Then have students color the page. When finished, allow time for them to share their answers with other students at the center.

Unit 2
Community Workers

Introductory Lesson—Part B

Objectives

Pre-K Standard 5.11: Students use emergent reading skills to "read" a story (e.g., gather meaning from words and pictures).

K–2 Standard 7.3: Students summarize information found in texts (e.g., retell in their own words).

Skills

- locating important facts in text
- recognizing important facts and less important facts
- identifying important facts by looking at pictures
- explaining important facts in their own words

Materials

- Social Studies Cards 14–17
- short article from a local newspaper that would be of interest to students
- chalk or whiteboard markers
- chalkboard or whiteboard

Word Study

- dentist
- healthy
- teeth
- sanitation worker
- clean
- nurse
- sick
- chef
- meals
- restaurant

Comprehension and Skills

Part 1: Lesson Length: approx. 15 minutes

1. Tell students you are going to read an article that has important information in it. Invite students to help you find the important information. Tell them to listen carefully as you read the article.

2. Read the article to students. After reading, ask students a question about the article that can be answered by reading it. Write the question on the board. Explain that not all of the information in the article will help answer this question. Read the article again and have students raise their hands when they hear information that might be helpful in answering the question on the board.

3. After reading, ask students to share any information they heard that will answer the question. Write their responses on the board. As a class, decide which responses best answer the question.

Introductory Lesson—Part B (cont.)

Comprehension and Skills

Part 2: Lesson Length: approx. 15 minutes

1. Distribute Social Studies Cards 14–17 to small groups of students and have them look for the important information. This might include the word at the top of the card and the sentence at the bottom. Review the vocabulary words. Come together as a whole class. Read the sentences on the cards aloud. Point out and emphasize the boldfaced words.

2. Have students close their eyes and visualize which community member you describe. If they know who you are describing, instruct students to raise their hands. Continue giving clues until a majority of students are raising their hands.

3. Describe a sanitation worker using the following clues:

   • This person drives a big truck.
   • This person has to smell a lot of bad smells.
   • This person helps to keep the neighborhood clean.
   • This person recycles things.

4. Once most students have determined whom you are talking about, ask them to open their eyes and share their ideas. Did they guess a sanitation worker? Point out that you gave students information and they were able to visualize who was being described. Students were listening for important facts that would help them figure out what you were talking about.

5. Continue this visualization activity for Social Studies Cards 15–17.

Assessment

Ask students how they used the clues you gave them to figure out that you were talking about a sanitation worker. Remind students that it is important to listen and read for important facts. Ask students to explain how they can locate important facts in what they read. How can they determine whether the information they are reading is important?

Give students a Social Studies Card that you have previously used in this unit. Using this card, have students share new information that they can learn from looking at the card. Encourage them to explain how this information can help them.

Unit 2
Community Workers

Focus Lesson

Objectives

Pre-K Standard 5.11: Students use emergent reading skills to "read" a story (e.g., gather meaning from words and pictures).

K–2 Standard 7.3: Students summarize information found in texts (e.g., retell in their own words).

Skills

- locating important facts in text
- recognizing important facts and less important facts
- identifying important facts by looking at pictures
- explaining important facts in their own words

Materials

- Social Studies Cards 15–17
- chalk or whiteboard markers
- chalkboard or whiteboard
- white paper for each student
- crayons, colored pencils, or markers

Word Study

- nurse
- sick
- dentist
- healthy
- teeth
- chef
- meals
- restaurant

Comprehension and Skills

Part 1: Lesson Length: approx. 20 minutes

1. Ask students to close their eyes and picture themselves walking into a doctor's office. Ask, "What do you see? What do you hear? What do you smell? What can you touch in the doctor's office? What words do you say?" Ask students to open their eyes and share their imaginary experiences.

2. Ask, "What types of workers are there at a doctor's office?" Explain that a nurse works in a doctor's office. A nurse can also work in a hospital, a school, and many other places.

3. Now hold up Social Studies Card 15 and ask students to read this card with you. Make the sound of the first letter in the word *nurse*. Then have students make the sounds for the rest of the remaining letters and sound out the word *nurse*. Now read the sentence at the bottom of the card, encouraging students to read the sentence with you. Point to each word as you read. Point out the capital letter at the beginning of the sentence and the period at the end of the sentence. Ask, "According to this card, what does a nurse do?"

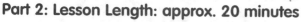

Focus Lesson (cont.)

Comprehension and Skills

Part 2: Lesson Length: approx. 20 minutes

1. Invite students to share experiences they have had going to the dentist. Ask, "Why do people go to a dentist? What do people do at the dentist's office?"

2. Hold up Social Studies Card 16 and invite students to read the word at the top of the card. Ask them what sound the first letter makes. Then make the sound for each of the remaining letters in the word *dentist*. Blend these sounds together to make the word *dentist*.

3. Ask students what *dentist* means. Play a game of charades by having one student at a time act out something that a dentist does. As students guess, make a list of these actions on the board. After the game, call students' attention to the list. Point out that a dentist does many different things. Hold up Social Studies Card 16 and ask, "What is the dentist trying to show to the little girl?" Talk about what we can learn from this card. Now read the sentence at the bottom of the card, pointing to each word as you read.

Comprehension and Skills

Part 3: Lesson Length: approx. 20 minutes

1. Hold up Social Studies Card 17. Ask students who the person in the picture is and where she is working. Talk about the woman's clothing and why she is dressed this way. Help students read the word *chef*. Ask students what they think a chef does. Have students read the sentence at the bottom of the card with you while pointing to each word. Ask them if their guesses regarding a chef were correct.

2. Ask students if they have ever been to a restaurant. Ask, "Did the restaurant look like the one on the card?"

3. Tell students that you would like to design your own menu. Brainstorm foods that would be on the menu and write these on the board. Then shorten the list by voting for the most popular foods. Be sure to have drinks, salads, appetizers, main dishes, and desserts. Give students paper and have them design pictures for the menu.

Time to Differentiate!

For above-level students, allow them to work in small groups to create their own menus for a restaurant. You may wish to give each group a large sheet of chart paper to work with.

Assessment

Ask students to explain what dentists, nurses, and chefs do. Have students explain where they got the information about these community workers. Explain that we can get information from a variety of places.

Unit 2
Community Workers

Center Activities

Objectives

Pre-K Standard 5.11: Students use emergent reading skills to "read" a story (e.g., gather meaning from words and pictures).

K–2 Standard 7.3: Students summarize information found in texts (e.g., retell in their own words).

Center #1:
Keeping Our Streets Clean

Materials

- Social Studies Card 14
- student copies of Activity 14 (page 102)
- map of your city or town
- crayons or colored pencils

Comprehension and Skills

1. Hold up Social Studies Card 14. Together, read the words *sanitation worker*, as well as the sentence at the bottom of the page. Review the definition of a sanitation worker.

2. Display a map of your city or town. Explain that this map is a picture of where we live. Point out where sanitation workers need to go to pick up trash, including your school. Discuss how sanitation workers get their work done.

3. Distribute copies of Activity 14 (page 102). Read the directions at the top of the page. Instruct students to circle all the objects in the picture that the sanitation worker should put in his truck. Then ask students to color the picture.

Center #2:
Dentists and Nurses

Materials

- Social Studies Cards 15–16
- student copies of Activities 15 and 16 (pages 103 and 104)
- crayons, scissors, and glue
- magazines
- white paper

Comprehension and Skills

1. Display Social Studies Cards 15 and 16. Ask the following questions:
   - How are a nurse and a dentist similar?
   - How are a nurse and a dentist different?
   - How are the clothes the nurse and the dentist are wearing similar?
   - How do they help you to be healthy?

2. Distribute copies of Activity 15 (page 103). Read the directions. Have students draw a line from each item to the nurse.

3. Distribute copies of Activity 16 (page 104). Instruct students to color each tooth that has advice below it that a dentist might give you. Have them explain why a dentist would not say some of the phrases on this page.

4. At the center, give students magazines. Instruct them to look through the magazines and cut out pictures of people that a dentist or a nurse might help. Glue the pictures onto a sheet of paper. Students can then draw a picture of a nurse or dentist helping these people.

Center Activities *(cont.)*

Center #3:
Yummy Recipes

Materials

- Social Studies Card 17
- student copies of Activity 17 (page 105)
- crayons or colored pencils

Comprehension and Skills

1. Hold up Social Studies Card 17 and ask, "What is the woman in this picture doing? Can you tell what she is cooking?" Read the sentence at the bottom of the card with students. Ask them to locate the word *chef* in the sentence.

2. Distribute copies of Activity 17 (page 105) and read the directions at the top of the page. When students have finished their recipes, have them each draw a picture of their favorite food on the back of the page.

3. Once students have completed their work, invite them to share their recipes and drawings with the class. Compare and contrast the foods and recipes. Ask students if they have ever prepared these foods before.

4. Collect all of the recipes and pictures and bind them into a cookbook. These recipes and directions are creative and can be used as gifts for special occasions.

Unit 2
Community Workers

Wrap-up

Introduction

The wrap-up activities tie together the skills that have been taught throughout the unit. They provide opportunities for students to show the skills they have learned within this unit.

Objectives

Pre-K Standard 5.11: Students use emergent reading skills to "read" a story (e.g., gather meaning from words and pictures).

Pre-K Standard 5.13: Students use visual and verbal cues, including pictures, to comprehend new words and stories.

K–2 Standard 6.4: Students know the main ideas or themes of a story.

K–2 Standard 7.3: Students summarize information found in texts (e.g., retell in their own words).

Materials

- Social Studies Cards 10–17
- student copies of page 97
- crayons, markers, or colored pencils
- magazines
- scissors
- glue

Comprehension and Skills

1. If possible, set up a career day and invite members of your community who hold the same jobs as the people studied on the cards. Encourage the guests to demonstrate or provide examples of their work. After each guest speaks, ask students to clarify main points that the guest mentioned.

2. As a class, browse through a phone book to locate a person or an organization that is affiliated with each of the jobs mentioned on Social Studies Cards 10–17. Then discuss this activity with students. Ask, "How is the information in the phone book helpful? How can you find the information you need in a phone book?"

3. Once students have learned about the variety of jobs in the community, ask them to think about the type of job that they would each like to have when they grow up. Is this job one of those spotlighted on Social Studies Cards 10–17? Have students cut out magazine pictures that show a person doing a job that the student likes or pictures of tools that person might use.

4. Distribute copies of page 97. Have students glue their magazine pictures to their activity pages. If desired, a class book can be created with the student pages. Store this book in the class library for future reference.

Community Workers

Finish the sentence below. Paste the pictures that you found. Show the jobs you would like to do.

When I grow up, I want to be a . . .

Unit 2
Community Workers

Put a check [✓] in front of each job a **teacher** might do at school. Then add another job your **teacher** does.

[   ] read a book   [   ] collect lunch money

[   ] sing a song   [   ] check homework

[   ] ride a bike   [   ] walk the dog

[   ] do laundry   [   ] use the computer

[   ] write a story

Color the clothing that a **firefighter** would wear.

How does a **police officer** get around the neighborhood? Circle the ways.

What might this **crossing guard** be saying? Write the words in the speech balloon.

Help the **sanitation worker** do his job. Circle all the things in the picture that the worker should put in his truck.

Help this **nurse** pack her bag. Draw a line from each thing the nurse needs to her bag.

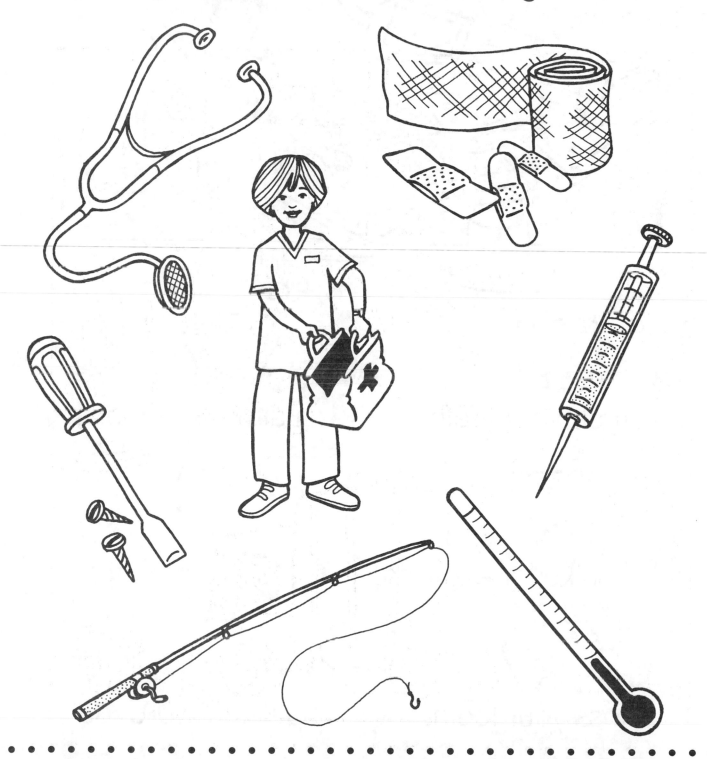

Unit 2
Community Workers

Color each tooth that tells advice a **dentist** might give you.

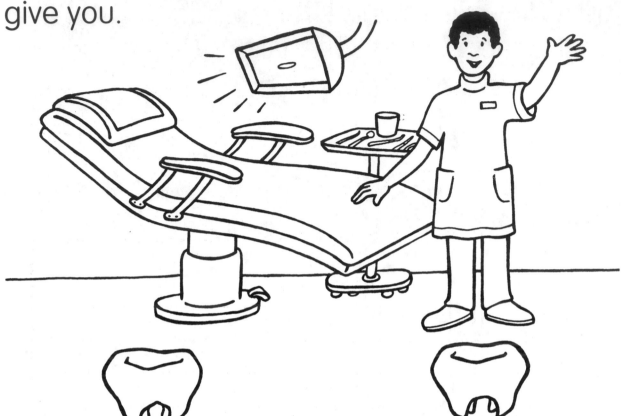

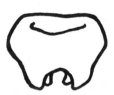

Brush your teeth.

Eat healthy foods.

Ride a bike for exercise.

Visit your dentist.

Floss your teeth.

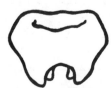

Spell the word tooth.

Help this **chef** cook something special. Write the name of the food on the recipe card. Then list the ingredients and the steps.

Recipe card

_____
_____
_____
_____
_____
_____
_____
_____
_____
_____
_____

My Community

Community Workers

Kinds of Land and Water

The United States

Introduction to Unit 3: Kinds of Land and Water

In this essential social studies unit, students will learn the difference between different bodies of water and land formations. Important vocabulary terms such as *plain*, *river*, *ocean*, *hill*, *lake*, and *land* are introduced. Students will learn that illustrations and photographs convey meaning. Also, students will learn to organize content knowledge to answer a specific question.

Skills Taught in This Unit

- identifying illustrations and photographs
- identifying differences between illustrations and photographs
- recognizing the meanings behind illustrations and photographs
- identifying the main idea by looking at pictures
- identifying content knowledge from text
- using content knowledge to answer questions about text
- brainstorming background knowledge
- understanding the main idea

Directions for the Teacher

You have many different options when teaching this unit. You can use the nonfiction text pages (Social Studies Cards) and teach the content using the strategies that precede each text passage. Or, you can teach nonfiction skills and strategies by teaching the whole unit, starting with the introductory lesson, then teaching the focus lesson, and then following up with the center activities. This format repeats for the second lesson in the unit. Conclude the unit by teaching the wrap-up activity to tie all the nonfiction text and skills together.

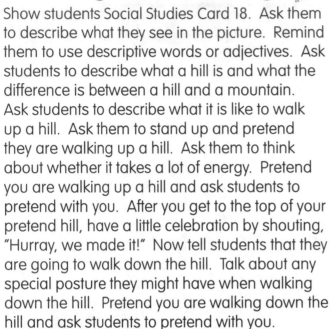

Unit 3
Kinds of Land and Water

Activating Prior Knowledge

Show students Social Studies Card 18. Ask them to describe what they see in the picture. Remind them to use descriptive words or adjectives. Ask students to describe what a hill is and what the difference is between a hill and a mountain. Ask students to describe what it is like to walk up a hill. Ask them to stand up and pretend they are walking up a hill. Ask them to think about whether it takes a lot of energy. Pretend you are walking up a hill and ask students to pretend with you. After you get to the top of your pretend hill, have a little celebration by shouting, "Hurray, we made it!" Now tell students that they are going to walk down the hill. Talk about any special posture they might have when walking down the hill. Pretend you are walking down the hill and ask students to pretend with you.

Language Development

Ask students to look at the card and describe what they see. Direct their attention to the word *hill* at the top of the card. Tell them the word is *hill* and ask them if they can tell you what it begins with. After they respond, ask them to practice making the /h/ sound. Write the word *hill* on the board or a sheet of chart paper. Write the word with the "h" separated from the "-ill." Segment the word "h-ill," and ask students to repeat after you. Tell students that together you are going to make words that rhyme with the word *hill* by changing the beginning sound. Write a few examples on the board, such as *bill*, *will*, and *fill*. Direct students' attention to the sentence at the bottom of the card. Ask them if they recognize any words in the sentence. While pointing to the words, read the sentence. Ask students to read the sentence with you while you point to the words.

Building Knowledge and Comprehension

Ask students to look at the card again. Read the word *hill* at the top of the card and read the sentence at the bottom of the card. Before doing this activity, write the nursery rhyme "Jack and Jill Went up the Hill" on the board or a sheet of chart paper large enough for the class to see well. Ask students if they know any nursery rhymes that have the word *hill* in them. Remind them of the rhyme about Jack and Jill. Ask them what it was that Jack and Jill went up. Show students the Jack and Jill nursery rhyme and ask them if they recognize any words. Highlight any words that students recognize or any words that you want them to focus on. Point to the words as you read the rhyme several times with students. Have students take turns pointing to the words while the remainder of the class reads them aloud. Ask students to draw a picture of a hill and label it.

Time to Differentiate!

For English language learners, preteach the vocabulary needed for the Building Knowledge and Comprehension lesson. Show students pictures of a pail, water, etc. Say each word as you show the picture, and then ask students to repeat it.

For below-level students, provide choices for the rhyming activity in the Language Development lesson. For example, ask students, "Which word rhymes with *hill—bill* or *back*?

hill

A **hill** is land that rises up.

Activating Prior Knowledge

Show students Social Studies Card 19. Ask them to describe what they see using adjectives or describing words. Tell them that the picture is of a mountain. Ask if any students have ever been to the mountains. Allow time for students to share their experiences. Some students may have never been to the mountains. Ask them to think about what the experience might be like, based on what other classmates have shared. Ask them to think about the activities a person can do in the mountains. Give students time to share their ideas with the rest of the class. Write the students' ideas on the board or a sheet of chart paper. Give students a few ideas, such as hiking, biking, camping, and skiing. Ask volunteers to act out each of these activities. Ask them what season it should be for each activity and what special equipment is needed.

Language Development

Ask students to look at the card and describe what they see. Direct their attention to the word *mountain* at the top of the card. Tell them the word is *mountain* and ask them if they can tell you what it begins with. After they tell you it begins with the letter "m," ask them to practice making the /m/ sound. Tell students you are going to say the word *mountain* and you want them to listen closely and then tell you what sound they hear at the end of the word. After they respond, ask them to practice making the /n/ sound. Direct students' attention to the sentence at the bottom of the card. Ask them if they recognize any words in the sentence. While pointing to the words, read the sentence. Ask students to read the sentence with you while you point to the words. While reading the sentence, have students raise their hands high when you read the word *mountain*.

Building Knowledge and Comprehension

Ask students to look at the card and describe what they see. Discuss with students the difference between a mountain and a hill. Tell them you are going to make mountains out of clay or baker's dough (recipe follows). Model for students how to make a mountain out of the clay or baker's dough. Give each child a large ball of dough and a piece of tinfoil to build it on. When they are finished building their mountain, let the clay dry or bake the baker's dough. Have students paint and decorate their mountains.

Directions: To make baker's dough, you will need the following ingredients: 1 cup flour, 1/2 cup salt, and 1/2 cup water. Put flour and salt in mixing bowl. Mix well. Add water slowly until the flour and salt make a stiff dough consistency. Each recipe makes dough for one student. Make into shapes. Bake at 300 degrees for approximately 45 minutes. Let cool completely before painting.

Time to Differentiate!

For English language learners, help them build background knowledge by introducing key words and concepts. Explain and act out hiking, biking, camping, and skiing. Then repeat the words and concepts and ask students to act them out with you.

For below-level students, scaffold the discussion activities by encouraging them to talk with partners before sharing their thoughts or experiences with the class. If needed, model for them how to answer in complete sentences.

mountain

A **mountain** is the highest kind of land.

Activating Prior Knowledge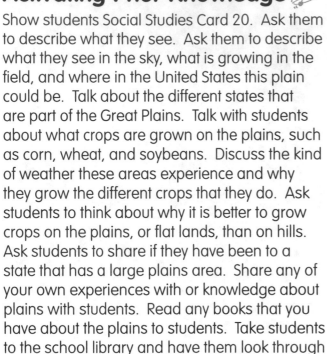

Show students Social Studies Card 20. Ask them to describe what they see. Ask them to describe what they see in the sky, what is growing in the field, and where in the United States this plain could be. Talk about the different states that are part of the Great Plains. Talk with students about what crops are grown on the plains, such as corn, wheat, and soybeans. Discuss the kind of weather these areas experience and why they grow the different crops that they do. Ask students to think about why it is better to grow crops on the plains, or flat lands, than on hills. Ask students to share if they have been to a state that has a large plains area. Share any of your own experiences with or knowledge about plains with students. Read any books that you have about the plains to students. Take students to the school library and have them look through a variety of books about the plains.

Language Development

Ask students to look at the card and describe what they see. Direct their attention to the word *plain* at the top of the card. Tell them the word is *plain* and ask them if they can tell you what it begins with. After they respond, ask them to practice making the /pl/ blend. Tell students you are going to say the word *plain* and you want them to listen closely and then tell you what sound they hear at the end of the word. After they respond, ask them to practice making the /n/ sound. Direct students' attention to the sentence at the bottom of the card. Ask students if they recognize any words in the sentence. While pointing to the words, read the sentence. Ask students to read the sentence with you while you point to the words. While reading the sentence, have students clap their hands when you read the word *plain*.

Building Knowledge and Comprehension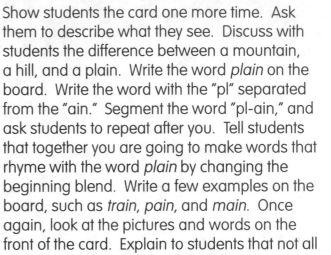

Show students the card one more time. Ask them to describe what they see. Discuss with students the difference between a mountain, a hill, and a plain. Write the word *plain* on the board. Write the word with the "pl" separated from the "ain." Segment the word "pl-ain," and ask students to repeat after you. Tell students that together you are going to make words that rhyme with the word *plain* by changing the beginning blend. Write a few examples on the board, such as *train, pain,* and *main.* Once again, look at the pictures and words on the front of the card. Explain to students that not all plains look like this one. Read aloud *Bringing the Rain to Kapiti Plain: A Nandi Tale,* retold by Verna Aardema. This is a rhyming book rich in colorful illlustrations. Have students draw pictures showing their favorite part of the book.

Time to Differentiate!

For English language learners, preview the book *Bringing the Rain to Kapiti Plain: A Nandi Tale.* Point out and discuss any key words and concepts. Show students the pictures as you describe them.

For below-level students, scaffold the rhyming activity in the Building Knowledge and Comprehension lesson. For example, ask students, "Which word rhymes with *plain—rain* or *penny*?

plain

A **plain** is land that is mostly flat.

Activating Prior Knowledge

Show students Social Studies Card 21. Ask them to describe what they see. Ask students to share some activities that a person could do on a lake. List the activities students suggest on the board or a sheet of chart paper. Some examples include boating, rafting, fishing, swimming, and waterskiing. Ask students to think about what animals live in or around a lake. Add their ideas to the board or chart paper. Talk about the words that you have written. Ask students to share any experiences they may have had at a lake. Share any experiences you have had at a lake. Read books that you have about lakes to students. Ask students to think about other types of bodies of water, such as rivers, oceans, and ponds. Ask students to think about what makes a lake different from these other types of water. Show pictures of these other water types, if possible.

Language Development

Ask students to look at the card and describe what they see. Direct their attention to the word *lake* at the top of the card. Tell them the word is *lake* and ask them if they can tell you what it begins with. After they respond, ask them to practice making the /l/ sound. Ask students what sound they hear at the end of the word. After they respond, practice making the /k/ sound. Point out that even though the last sound we hear is the /k/ sound, the word actually ends in "e." Explain the silent "e" rule, and how the letter "e" makes the "a" say its name. Direct students' attention to the sentence at the bottom of the card. Ask them if they recognize any words in the sentence. While pointing to the words, read the sentence. Ask students to read the sentence with you while you point to the words.

Building Knowledge and Comprehension

Discuss with students the difference between a lake environment and a plains environment. Ask students if lakes can only be in mountainous areas, like in the picture, or if can they be in other places. Show students a map of your state or country. Point out what a lake looks like on the map. Provide a water center for students to pretend they are at a lake. Use large rubber or plastic buckets. They should be large enough so two to four students can play at them at a time. Fill the buckets half full of water. Provide water toys for students to play with at each center, such as the following: measuring cups, spoons, small pitchers and cups, or anything that will create interest. Allow students to play at the center periodically throughout the day. Change the water in the tubs every day. Ask students to draw pictures of things that might be found at a lake and display these pictures in the center.

Time to Differentiate!

For English language learners, build students' background knowledge prior to the lessons. Show students the card. Point to various things in the picture and name them. Ask students to repeat the words. Write those words on sticky notes and place them on the picture.

For below-level students, preview the card in a small group. Read the words at the top of the card and ask students to repeat them. While pointing to each word, read the sentence at the bottom of the card. Repeat this several times.

lake

A **lake** is water with land all around it.

Activating Prior Knowledge

Show students Social Studies Card 22. Ask them to describe what they see. Ask students to share some activities that a person could do on a river. List the activities on the board or a sheet of chart paper. Examples include canoeing, rafting, and fishing. Ask students to share any experiences they have had on a river. Show students a map of your state or country. Discuss what a river looks like on a map and what the major rivers are where you live. Ask them to find all the rivers in your state or country. Show students a map of the United States. Discuss some of the major rivers in the United States, such as the Mississippi River, the Arkansas River, and the Colorado River. Discuss the difference between a river and a lake. Make a Venn diagram to chart the differences. Draw two interconnecting circles and in the center where they overlap, write the similarities. In the outer sections, write the differences.

Language Development

Ask students to look at the card and describe what they see. Direct their attention to the word *river* at the top of the card. Tell them the word is *river* and ask them if they can tell you what it begins with. After they respond, ask them to practice making the /r/ sound. Ask students what sound they hear at the end of the word. After they respond, ask them to practice making the /er/ sound. Be sure they notice that *river* begins and ends with the same letter. Direct students' attention to the sentence at the bottom of the card. Ask them if they recognize any words in the sentence. While pointing to the words, read the sentence. Ask students to read the sentence with you. While reading the sentence, have students pretend to row a boat when they hear the word *river*.

Building Knowledge and Comprehension

Show students the card. Ask them to describe what they see. Ask them to read the word *river* at the top of the card as you point to it. Ask them to read the sentence at the bottom of the card as you point to it. Discuss with students how rivers always flow toward an ocean. Even if the land appears to be perfectly flat, the river is still flowing toward an ocean somewhere. Ask students to think about where a river ends. If possible, make a small class river. Find a dirt area or sand box containing coarse sand. Take students out to the playground. First determine which way the river is going to flow. Give each student a digging toy. Tongue depressors, craft sticks, or plastic spoons will work if you don't have enough digging toys for all students. If possible, ask each student to bring a digging toy (labeled with his or her name) from home to use. Begin to dig a river. When your riverbed has been dug, pour water in it at one end and discuss which way the water is flowing.

Time to Differentiate!

For English language learners, preview the map of the United States. Point to and label the major rivers. Then repeat each of the names and ask various students to point them out on the map.

For below-level students, preteach the /er/ sound. Name several words that feature the /er/ sound and have students repeat them.

river

A **river** is water that moves fast or slow through the land.

Unit 3
Kinds of Land and Water

ocean

Activating Prior Knowledge

Show students Social Studies Card 23. Ask them to describe what they see. Ask students if any of them have ever taken a trip to the ocean and ask them to share their experience with the class. Share any experiences you may have had. Show students a globe and discuss what oceans look like on the globe. Ask them if oceans are big or small. Discuss with them the fact that there is very little land compared to water on our planet. Illustrate this fact by pointing it out on the globe. Discuss what animals live in the ocean. List the animals students suggest on the board or a sheet of chart paper. Ask students to close their eyes and try to picture the ocean. What do they see? What do they hear? What do they smell? What do they taste? What do they feel? Read any books you may have about the ocean (e.g., *A House for Hermit Crab* by Eric Carle).

Language Development

Ask students to look at the card and describe what they see. Direct their attention to the word *ocean* at the top of the card. Tell them the word is *ocean* and ask them if they can tell you what it begins with. After they tell you it begins with the letter "o," ask them to practice making the long /ō/ sound. Talk with students about how, in this case, the "o" is making the long /ō/ sound. Tell students you are going to say the word *ocean* and you want them to listen closely and then tell you what sound they hear at the end of the word. After they respond, ask them to practice making the /n/ sound. Direct students' attention to the sentence at the bottom of the card. Ask students if they recognize any words in the sentence. While pointing to the words, read the sentence. Ask students to read the sentence with you while you point to the words.

Building Knowledge and Comprehension

Show students the card. Ask them to describe what they see. Ask them to read the word *ocean* at the top of the card as you point to it. Ask them to read the sentence at the bottom of the card as you point to it. Discuss with students the difference between a lake and an ocean. Is the water different in a lake than in an ocean? Ask students to help you make a list of animals that live in the ocean. Write the names of the animals students suggest on the board. Some examples are the following: whale, shark, stingray, and clown fish. Make a class book that follows the same pattern as *Brown Bear, Brown Bear*, by Bill Martin, Jr. For example, "Stingray, stingray, what do you see? I see a blue whale looking at me. Blue whale, blue whale, what do you see? I see a great white shark looking at me." Bind the book and have it displayed in the classroom for students to read together.

Time to Differentiate!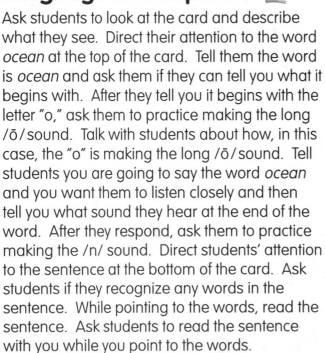

For English language learners, allow them time to draw a picture of an ocean animal. Then label their pictures in English. Show each student's picture and say the animal's name as you point to the word on the page.

For below-level students, help them hear the rhythm of the language in the class book you create. As you read the book, encourage students to clap to the "beat." You may also wish to include gestures or actions to certain words.

ocean

The **ocean** is salty water that covers much of the earth.

Unit 3
Kinds of Land and Water

Introductory Lesson—Part A

Objectives

Pre-K Standard 5.3: Students understand that illustrations and pictures convey meaning.

K–2 Standard 5.1: Students use mental images based on pictures and print to aid in comprehension of text.

Skills

- identifying illustrations and photographs
- identifying differences between illustrations and photographs
- recognizing the meanings behind illustrations and photographs
- identifying the main idea by looking at pictures

Materials

- Social Studies Cards 18–23
- photograph and illustration from a book or magazine
- various pictures cut from magazines (e.g., cake, ice cream cone, chair, dog)
- index cards with words that correspond to the pictures
- chalkboard or whiteboard
- chalk or whiteboard markers

Word Study

- hill
- rises
- plain
- mostly
- mountain
- highest
- lake
- land
- around
- river
- moves
- ocean
- salty
- covers

Comprehension and Skills

Part 1: Lesson Length: approx. 20 minutes

1. Hold up a picture from a magazine. Ask students to tell you what is going on in the picture. For example, hold up a picture of an animal. Ask students, "By looking at this picture, what can you tell me about this animal? Where does it live? What do you think it eats? What color is it? What type of skin or fur does it have? What does this animal do?" As students share information, record their observations and speculations on the board. When you have finished, read the student responses. Point to each word as you read. Ask students how they knew what was happening in the picture even though there were no words and you did not give them any background information. Explain that illustrations and photographs convey meaning to the reader.

2. Discuss the importance of pictures in reading. Pictures can usually tell us much more than words can. Pictures can clarify what the words are saying.

3. Discuss the differences between an illustration and a photograph. Show students samples of each, and then have them search the room for examples.

4. Hold up Social Studies Cards 18–23. Have students look at each card and think about what these pictures show. Ask, "What do you think the words might be saying?" Allow them to share what the cards and pictures remind them of. Read the text on the cards to the students, pointing to each word as you read it.

Introductory Lesson—Part A (cont.)

Comprehension and Skills

Part 2: Lesson Length: approx. 20 minutes

1. Cut out various magazine pictures. Write the names of each picture on an index card.

2. Take the pictures and post them on the board. Mix up the index cards with the corresponding words and post them on the other side of the board. As a class, try to match the words with the pictures. (You will need to assist students in sounding out words. You may wish to keep the words as simple as possible.)

3. Once all of the pictures and words have been matched, discuss the importance of the pictures. Tell students that the pictures helped them to understand the words that they were reading. Explain that pictures will help students read. Reading requires us to look at pictures to determine the words. Remind students that illustrations and photographs convey meaning.

4. Hold up Social Studies Cards 18–23. As you hold up each card, have students say the word that corresponds to it. Explain that these pictures help explain the words. (You may choose to do this activity with cards used in the previous lessons.) Remind students that using pictures can help us understand and read the words.

Assessment

Show several examples of books with photos and illustrations to students and ask them to discuss how important these can be for a reader. Instruct students to tell you how photographs and illustrations help us understand what we read.

Unit 3
Kinds of Land and Water

Focus Lesson

Objectives

Pre-K Standard 5.3: Students understand that illustrations and pictures convey meaning.

K–2 Standard 5.1: Students use mental images based on pictures and print to aid in comprehension of text.

Skills

- identifying illustrations and photographs
- identifying differences between illustrations and photographs
- recognizing the meanings behind illustrations and photographs
- identifying the main idea by looking at pictures

Materials

- Social Studies Cards 18–20
- chalk or whiteboard markers
- chalkboard or whiteboard

Word Study

- hill
- rises
- mountain
- highest
- plain
- mostly
- flat

Comprehension and Skills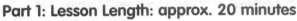

Part 1: Lesson Length: approx. 20 minutes

1. Begin this lesson by discussing the definition of a mountain. Encourage students to share their ideas about what a mountain is. How is a mountain different from a hill?

2. Hold up Social Studies Cards 18 and 19. By looking at the pictures, students should be able to determine the differences between a hill and a mountain. On the board write *hill* and *mountain*. Record students' observations under each column. When completed, point out how much information students were able to determine from the two pictures.

3. Sound out the word *mountain* that appears at the top of Social Studies Card 19. Read the sentence at the bottom of the card, pointing to each word as you go. Encourage students to state in their own words the definition of *mountain*. Repeat this procedure for Social Studies Card 18.

4. Using their bodies, have students demonstrate what a hill looks like. Then have them show what a mountain looks like.

Focus Lesson *(cont.)*

Comprehension and Skills

Part 2: Lesson Length: approx. 20 minutes

1. Begin the lesson by reviewing how photographs and illustrations can help readers understand what is being read. Tell students that there is a word that you would like help with. Hold up Social Studies Card 20 and ask students to look at the picture. Encourage them to tell you about everything they see in the picture. Record students' responses on the board. After observations have been made, ask students to help you sound out the word at the top of the page.

2. Using the appropriate student observations from the picture, explain the definition of the word *plain*. Then read the sentence at the bottom of the card, pointing to each word as you read. Ask students to speculate what grows on the plain by referring to the picture.

3. Have students demonstrate with their bodies what the plains would look like. Then have students show what a mountain looks like. Then have students show what a hill looks like. Each time you say "hill," "plain," or "mountain," students should demonstrate. Mix up the words to get them moving.

Time to Differentiate!

For above-level students, have them create skits to show different activities people can do at the various geographic features taught in this unit.

Assessment

Have students look at Social Studies Card 20 and read the word *plain* and the sentence from the bottom of the card. Then have students explain how the photograph on the card helps to understand the word *plain*.

Ask each student to tell you the meaning of the word *mountain*. Have Social Studies Card 19 available and encourage students to use the photograph and the words on this card to assist in their definitions.

Unit 3
Kinds of Land and Water

Center Activities

Objectives

Pre-K Standard 5.3: Students understand that illustrations and pictures convey meaning.

K–2 Standard 5.1: Students use mental images based on pictures and print to aid in comprehension of text.

Center #1: Building Hills

Materials

- Social Studies Card 18
- student copies of Activity 18 (page 134)
- crayons, colored pencils, or markers
- clay or modeling dough

Comprehension and Skills

1. Hold up Social Studies Card 18 and ask students to read the words on the card. Read the word *hill* together while reviewing the sounds of each letter.

2. Distribute copies of Activity 18 (page 134). Have students look at each of the pictures on this page. Discuss each of the pictures as a class. Have students find the picture with a hill and color it. Then have students trace the word *hill*.

3. At a center, have students use the clay or modeling dough to make hills. Have them make other shapes as well to show the difference between hills and other features. Finally, have them form the letters for *hill*. As you circulate, invite students to share their clay "pictures" and read the word.

Center #2: Mountain Symbols

Materials

- Social Studies Card 19
- student copies of Activity 19 (page 135)
- map of the United States
- crayons, colored pencils, or markers

Comprehension and Skills

1. Display a map of the United States. Explain that this map is a "picture" of the United States. Locate a specific state and the symbol for mountains. Have students help you locate mountain symbols on the map. Look at your state. Ask, "Are there any mountains close by? What are their names?"

2. Hold up Social Studies Card 19. Ask, "Do you think this mountain looks like it is located in the area where we live? Why or why not?" Read the word *mountain*. Point to each word in the sentence as you read.

3. Distribute copies of Activity 19 (page 135). Encourage students to identify the differences between this map and the map on the board. Read the directions. Help students find the words *Mount McKinley* on the map. Explain that this is the tallest mountain in the United States. Have students find other mountains on this map.

4. At the center, have students color their maps. Instruct students to color the mountains all the same color in order to create a symbol. Then have students to compare their maps with the map on the board.

Center Activities (cont.)

Center #3:
Great Plains Maps

Materials

- Social Studies Card 20
- student copies of Activity 20 (page 136)
- colored pencils, markers, or crayons

Comprehension and Skills

1. Distribute copies of Activity 20 (page 136). Explain that this is a picture of the United States. This picture is called a map and this map will give details about the United States. Hold up Social Studies Card 20 and ask students to sound out and read the word *plain*. Then read the sentence at the bottom of the card.

2. Tell students that the map they have shows the area in the United States that is called the Great Plains. Read the sentences at the top of Activity 20 and point to each word as you read. Have students point to the words in the sentences as you read.

3. At the center, have students color and complete their activity sheets. Ask students to use the color green when coloring the Great Plains on the map. Have students color the mountains brown and the river blue.

Unit 3
Kinds of Land and Water

Introductory Lesson—Part B

Objectives

Pre-K Standard 6.5: Students relate stories to their own lives and experiences.

K–2 Standard 7.4: Students relate new information to prior knowledge and experience.

Skills

- identifying content knowledge from text
- using content knowledge to answer questions about text
- brainstorming background knowledge
- understanding the main idea

Materials

- Social Studies Cards 21–23
- article from local newspaper
- short story of interest to students
- student copies of a different short story at an appropriate reading level
- chalk or whiteboard markers
- chalkboard or whiteboard

Word Study

- river
- moves
- fast
- slow
- ocean
- salty
- covers
- lake
- land
- around

Comprehension and Skills

Part 1: Lesson Length: approx. 20 minutes

1. Tell students you are going to read an article that has important information in it. Invite students to help you find the important information. Tell them to listen carefully as you read the article.

2. Read the article to students. After reading, ask students a question about the article that can be answered by reading it. Write the question on the board. Explain that not all of the information in the article will help answer this question. Read the article again and have students raise their hands when they hear information that might be helpful in answering the question on the board.

3. After reading, ask students to share any information they heard that will answer the question. Write their responses on the board. As a class, decide which responses best answer the question.

4. Distribute Social Studies Cards 21–23 to small groups of students. Have them look for and discuss the important information on the cards.

5. Individually ask students to tell you the meaning of the word *river*. Have Social Studies Card 22 available to use as needed. Encourage students to use the photograph and the words on this card to assist in their definitions.

Introductory Lesson—Part B *(cont.)*

Comprehension and Skills

Part 2: Lesson Length: approx. 20 minutes

1. Gather students in a circle and read a selected short story to them. At the end of the story, call on a student to ask a question that can be answered by reading the story. Record the student's question on the board. Ask students if they know where in the story the answer can be found. Give the book to a student volunteer to look for the answer. Allow the student time to locate the answer in the story. The student will be using words and pictures as clues. Once the answer in the story has been found, read the section that answers the question. Select another student to ask a question. Record this question and then call on volunteers to find the answer.

2. Explain to students that they have been organizing information in order to answer a specific question. Explain the importance of being able to locate the answer in the text.

3. Hold up Social Studies Cards 22 and 23 and ask students to locate where they think they will find information on these cards. Solicit predictions on what they think the cards are about. The pictures can help them determine the content as well as locate important information.

4. Have students "buddy read" an appropriately leveled short story, using the pictures to help figure out what is going on in the story. After the story has been read, have each student take a turn to ask questions about the story. Have the other student in the pair locate the answer to the question.

Assessment

Give each student a turn to hold up Social Studies Cards 22 and 23 and share what he or she knows about rivers and oceans. Encourage students to share information they have learned before this lesson; then have them share what they have learned since starting this lesson.

Unit 3
Kinds of Land and Water

Focus Lesson

Objectives

Pre-K Standard 6.5: Students relate stories to their own lives and experiences.

K–2 Standard 7.4: Students relate new information to prior knowledge and experience.

Skills

- identifying content knowledge from text
- using content knowledge to answer questions about text
- brainstorming background knowledge
- understanding the main idea

Materials

- Social Studies Cards 21–23
- chalk or whiteboard markers
- chalkboard or whiteboard
- white paper
- crayons
- watercolors and brushes

Word Study

- lake
- land
- around
- river
- moves
- fast
- slow
- ocean
- salty
- covers

Comprehension and Skills

Part 1: Lesson Length: approx. 20 minutes

1. Write the word *lake* on the board and have students brainstorm everything they know about lakes. Make a brainstorming web to record this information. If there is a lake in your area, encourage students to share information they know about it.

2. Show students Social Studies Card 21. Ask students to talk about what they can learn from the picture on this card. Then sound out the word *lake* with the class. Ask students to share their own definitions of a lake.

3. Have students join you in reading the sentence at the bottom of the card, pointing to each word as you read. Point out the period at the end of the sentence and the capital letter at the beginning.

4. Ask students, "What information on the card can help us know what a lake is?" Students should identify the word *lake* and the sentence at the bottom of the card. Both of these share relevant information.

5. Repeat this using Social Studies Card 22.

Focus Lesson (cont.)

Comprehension and Skills

Part 2: Lesson Length: approx. 30 minutes

1. Make a list on the board of items needed for going to the beach (e.g., swimsuit, towel, sunglasses, sunscreen, beach ball, snacks).

2. Ask students why they need these items at the beach. Ask, "What is the beach like? Why do we need these items at the beach?"

3. Ask students to show you what they do at the beach. Pair up students. One student acts as a statue while the other student moves the arms, legs, head, and hands of the "statue" to show what someone at the beach would look like. Then have students switch roles.

Comprehension and Skills

Part 3: Lesson Length: approx. 30 minutes

1. Meet in a circle with the whole class. Discuss with students why we make certain actions and do certain things at the beach. Give students paper and have them draw a picture of what they look like while at the beach. Then have them use watercolors to paint a picture of themselves at the beach.

2. Allow students to share their pictures in small groups. Ask, "What can we learn from these pictures about the beach and the ocean?" Encourage students to define the words *beach* and *ocean*. Record these definitions to use in Part 4 of this lesson. Read these definitions to the class and point to each word as you read. Explain to students that they were able to share information about the ocean by sharing what they know about the beach.

Comprehension and Skills

Part 4: Lesson Length: approx. 20 minutes

1. Show students Social Studies Card 23. Point to the word *ocean* as you read it. Discuss the card by using these questions:
   - What does the word *ocean* mean?
   - If you were in the picture, what would you be doing?
   - How would it would feel to be in the picture?

2. Chorally read the sentence at the bottom of the card. Point to each word as you read. Ask what information can be gathered about oceans from this sentence.

3. Make a bulletin board with the class using the pictures that students painted in Part 2 of this lesson. Be sure to spell *ocean* on the bulletin board to give students more practice reading the word.

4. Have each student act out something he or she can do in or around the ocean. Other students can guess the action. Continue until all students have had a turn.

Time to Differentiate!

For above-level students, have them create riddles to give clues about each geographic feature. Students can read their riddles to the class.

Assessment

Have students explain how to identify important information. Using students' pictures, have them explain the definition of *ocean*. Then ask them questions about the ocean. Ask, "How does the picture help answer these questions?"

Unit 3
Kinds of Land and Water

Center Activities

Objectives

Pre-K Standard 6.5: Students relate stories to their own lives and experiences.

K–2 Standard 7.4: Students relate new information to prior knowledge and experience.

Center #1:
Imagine a Day at the Lake

Materials

- Social Studies Card 21
- student copies of Activity 21 (page 137)
- colored pencils, markers, or crayons

Comprehension and Skills

1. Hold up Social Studies Card 21 and have students read the words on this card. Begin with the word *lake*. Sound out each letter, reminding students about the silent "e" rule to make the long /ā/ sound. Then read the sentence at the bottom of the page. Point to each word as you read. Ask students to explain if this sentence is helpful information and how they can tell what information is helpful.

2. Now have students close their eyes and picture themselves sitting on the edge of the lake pictured on the card. Encourage students to think about how it would feel to sit by the lake. Ask them, "How would it smell near a lake? What noises would you hear? What would the ground feel like? What would you eat? What else would you notice sitting by the lake?" Encourage students to share the pictures they have created in their minds.

3. Distribute copies of Activity 21 (page 137). Point out that this is a map of the United States. This map shows some of the lakes in the United States. Help students read the sentences at the top of the page, pointing to each word as you read. Review with students what they need to do with this page. Then have students count how many lakes are on the map.

4. At a center, have students color the lakes blue and then color the rest of the map using different colors. If there are lakes in your area, help students locate and color them. Then ask students to draw a picture of themselves at a lake.

5. Review the definition of a lake. Ask students how they can tell the difference between a lake and other bodies of water. What information is key to the definition of a lake that is not relevant when talking about other types of water? Hold up Social Studies Card 21 and read the sentence at the bottom of the card. Help students identify the important words that describe a lake.

Center Activities (cont.)

Center #2:
Rivers and Oceans

Materials
- Social Studies Cards 22 and 23
- student copies of Activities 22 and 23 (pages 138 and 139)
- social studies textbook
- colored pencils, markers, or crayons

Comprehension and Skills

1. Show Social Studies Card 22 to students. Have them sound out the word *river* at the top of the page. Then help students read the sentence at the bottom of the page. Review the definition of the word *river*. Point out that *river* is in boldfaced type. Explain that boldfaced lettering shows the reader that this is an important word.

2. Now show students the social studies textbook. Point out examples of boldfaced print. Explain that this style of lettering calls attention to the reader and lets the reader know that it is important.

3. Distribute copies of Activity 22 (page 138). Ask students to find the boldfaced lettering on the page. Ask them to tell you why this word is in boldfaced print. Now read the directions on this page.

4. Have students complete this activity at a center. Students are to color the Mississippi River blue. Encourage them to color the rest of the map with colors of their own choosing. Remind them not to use the color blue for anything other than identifying a river on the map. If you are located in an area near a river, direct students to use the color blue to add it to the map. If you live near a river, ask students to talk about what it is like to live close to a river. Ask, "What is a river like?" Instruct students to draw a picture of themselves near a river on the bottom of their activity sheets. Have them depict what they are doing. What else is near the river? Allow time for students to share their work with the class, comparing and contrasting their drawings.

5. Show Social Studies Card 23 to students. Have them sound out the word *ocean*. Then help students read the sentence at the bottom of the page. Review the definition of the word *ocean*.

6. Distribute copies of Activity 23 (page 139). Read the sentences at the top of the page, pointing to each word as you read. Instruct students to use blue to color each ocean and brown to color the land on the map. Check for understanding by asking them how they are going to tell what part is ocean and what is land. Discuss as a class the differences between a river and an ocean.

Unit 3
Kinds of Land and Water

Wrap-up

Introduction

The wrap-up activities tie together the skills that have been taught throughout the unit. They provide opportunities for students to show the skills they have learned within this unit.

Objectives

Pre-K Standard 5.3: Students understand that illustrations and pictures convey meaning.

Pre-K Standard 6.5: Students relate stories to their own lives and experiences.

K–2 Standard 5.1: Students use mental images based on pictures and print to aid in comprehension of text.

K–2 Standard 7.4: Students relate new information to prior knowledge and experience.

Materials

- Social Studies Cards 18–23
- map of the world
- pictures of mountains, lakes, rivers, hills, plains, and oceans
- student copies of page 133

Comprehension and Skills

1. Post the pictures of the different types of land and water throughout the room. Invite students to walk around the room and look at the pictures. When they get to each picture, have them stop to determine the kind of land or water form pictured, as well as the meaning of the picture.

2. As a class, discuss the different types of land and water forms. Ask students to share how they knew what the pictures were depicting. Mix up Social Studies Cards 18–23. Hold up one card at a time and call on students to look around the room and find a picture that corresponds with the picture on the card. Continue until all students have had an opportunity to locate a picture on the wall that corresponds to each card. Explain to students that they are using the pictures to convey meaning. Have students analyze each picture and then return to their seats to complete the student activity (page 133).

3. Hang a map of the world in the classroom and invite groups of students to look at the map. Point out different types of land and water forms represented on the map, such as rivers, mountains, and oceans. Then ask students to find other oceans, rivers, and mountains on the map. Explain that they are organizing knowledge to answer a specific question.

4. Play the "What Am I?" game. Use the definitions from Social Studies Cards 18–23 to give clues to see if students can guess what kind of land or water form you are describing. This game will provide practice in organizing knowledge to answer a specific question.

Kinds of Land and Water

Sound out the words in each box. Draw a picture of the different types of land and water forms.

hill	plain	mountain
lake	**river**	**ocean**

Unit 3
Kinds of Land and Water

Name _____

Find the **hill**. Color and label it.

Trace the word.

Name _____

Mount McKinley in Alaska is the highest **mountain** in the United States. Can you find it? Circle Mount McKinley.

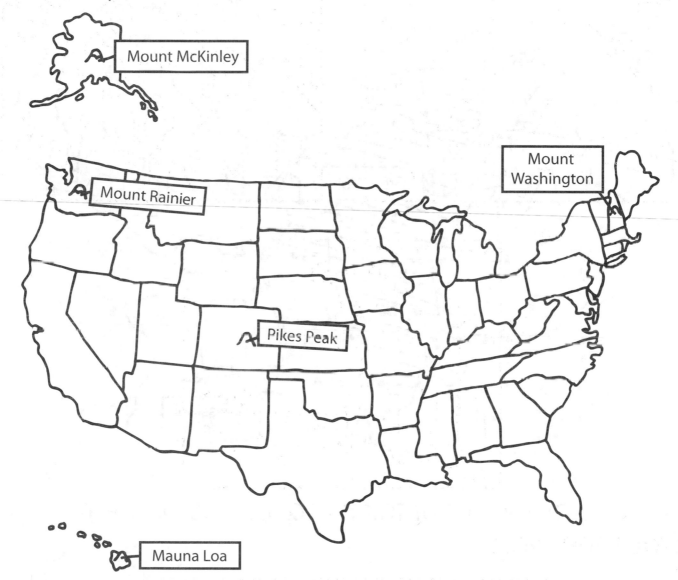

Mount McKinley

Mount Washington

Mount Rainier

Pikes Peak

Mauna Loa

Color all the mountains the same color to make a symbol. Color the rest of the map a different color.

The United States has an area of **plains** called the Great Plains. Color the Great Plains green.

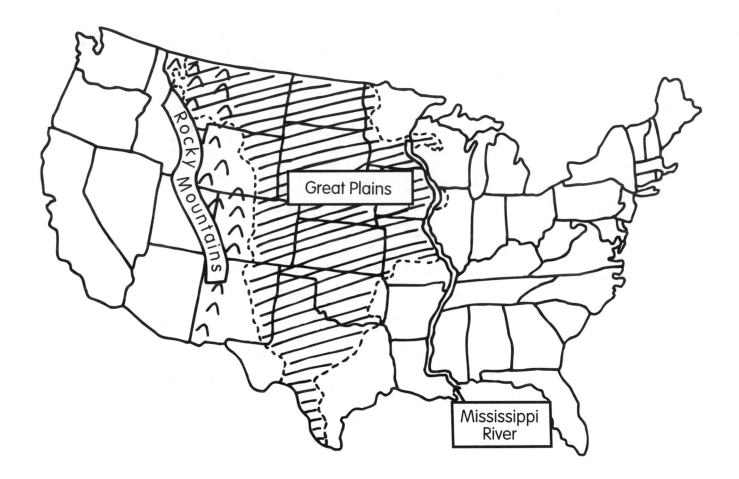

Now color the mountains brown. Color the river blue.

Name _____

Unit 3

Kinds of Land and Water

The United States has a set of five **lakes** called the Great Lakes. Color the Great Lakes blue.

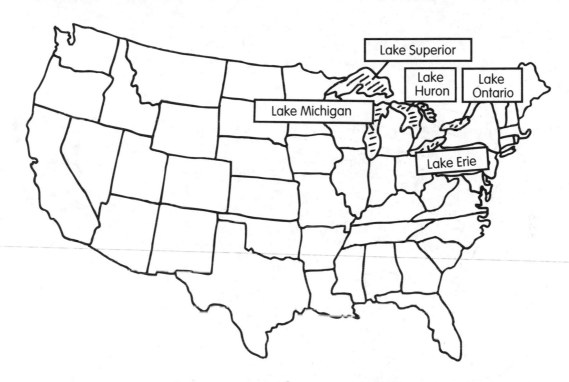

Draw a picture of yourself at a **lake**.

The Mississippi River is the longest **river** in the United States. Color it blue.

Mississippi River

Draw a picture of yourself at a **river**.

Name _____

Color each **ocean** on the world map blue. Color the land brown.

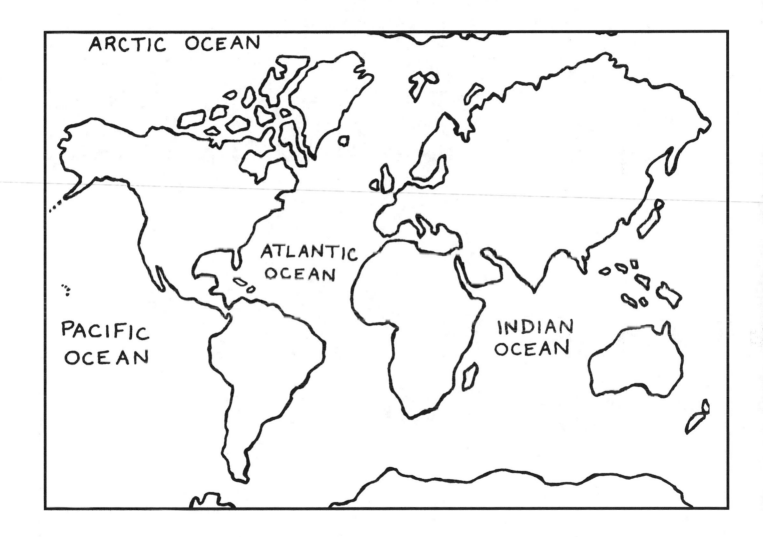

My Community

Community Workers

Kinds of Land and Water

The United States

Introduction to Unit 4: The United States

The United States is a theme that takes students on a journey through America, focusing on an exploration of important symbols such as the flag and the Capitol building. Important vocabulary terms such as *pledge, allegiance, nation, indivisible, liberty,* and *justice* are introduced. In this unit, students will learn to connect the information and events in the texts they read to life experience. Students will also learn to differentiate between thought-provoking questions and clarifying questions.

Skills Taught in This Unit

- identifying life experiences
- connecting life experiences to text events
- locating information in text
- recognizing larger thought-provoking questions
- recognizing smaller clarification questions
- determining the difference between larger and smaller questions about text

Directions for the Teacher

You have many different options when teaching this unit. You can use the nonfiction text pages (Social Studies Cards) and teach the content using the strategies that precede each text passage. Or, you can teach nonfiction skills and strategies by teaching the whole unit, starting with the introductory lesson, then teaching the focus lesson, and then following up with the center activities. This format repeats for the second lesson in the unit. Conclude the unit by teaching the wrap-up activity to tie all the nonfiction text and skills together.

Activating Prior Knowledge

Show students Social Studies Card 24. Ask them to describe what they see. Point out the flag in the classroom. Ask them to think about why each country has a flag and why we should respect it. Tell students to look at the stars and the stripes. Ask them if they know how many stars and stripes there are and why. Tell them that there are 50 stars and 13 stripes. The 50 stars represent the 50 states in the United States, and the 13 stripes represent the 13 original colonies that were present when the United States was founded. Discuss a few simple rules of etiquette for the flag. The flag should be displayed from sunrise to sunset and properly folded when taken down. If the weather is poor, the flag should not be displayed. It is a general rule that the flag is never to touch the ground because the ground is considered dirty.

Language Development

Tell students to look at the card and describe what they see. Talk about the word *flag*. Ask students if they can tell you what the word begins with. After they respond, ask them to practice making the /f/ sound. Talk about how the beginning sound in *flag* is really /fl/ and that these two letters together make a blend. Have students practice making the /fl/ blend. Then ask them to listen to the word *flag* as you say it out loud. Tell them to listen for the sound that they hear at the end of the word. Ask students if they can read any of the words in the sentence. Discuss any words that they recognize. While pointing to the words, read the sentence. Tell students to think of an action they could show when they read the word *flag*, such as saluting. Read the sentence again, having students make the agreed-upon action.

Building Knowledge and Comprehension

Ask students to look at the card again. Ask them to tell you what they already know about the flag. Ask students if they have any idea why the flag is red, white, and blue. Tell them it is this way for very specific reasons. Each color on the flag represents something. The red on the flag represents sacrifice, for all the sacrifices both military personnel and civilians have made to keep the Unites States free. Blue represents justice and how the Unites States was founded on the idea that all people will be treated fairly. White represents the idea of faith and purity and the idea that people will live lives full of honesty and integrity. Give each student a sheet of white construction paper and a red and blue crayon to draw an American flag. When they have finished making their flags, have students take them home to display.

Time to Differentiate!

For English language learners, help them build background knowledge by introducing key words and concepts. Explain and act out raising the flag, folding the flag, and keeping the flag off the ground. Then repeat the words and concepts and ask students to act them out with you.

For below-level students, scaffold the discussion activities by encouraging them to talk with partners before sharing their thoughts or experiences with the class. If needed, model for them how to answer in complete sentences.

flag

50 stars

13 stripes

This is the **flag** of the United States of America.

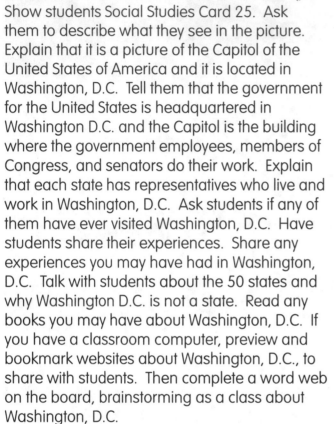
Activating Prior Knowledge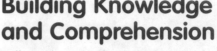

Show students Social Studies Card 25. Ask them to describe what they see in the picture. Explain that it is a picture of the Capitol of the United States of America and it is located in Washington, D.C. Tell them that the government for the United States is headquartered in Washington D.C. and the Capitol is the building where the government employees, members of Congress, and senators do their work. Explain that each state has representatives who live and work in Washington, D.C. Ask students if any of them have ever visited Washington, D.C. Have students share their experiences. Share any experiences you may have had in Washington, D.C. Talk with students about the 50 states and why Washington D.C. is not a state. Read any books you may have about Washington, D.C. If you have a classroom computer, preview and bookmark websites about Washington, D.C., to share with students. Then complete a word web on the board, brainstorming as a class about Washington, D.C.

Language Development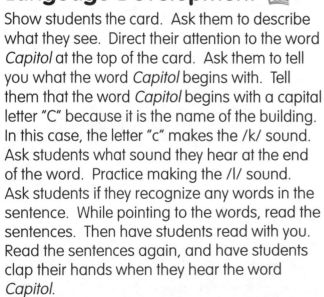

Show students the card. Ask them to describe what they see. Direct their attention to the word *Capitol* at the top of the card. Ask them to tell you what the word *Capitol* begins with. Tell them that the word *Capitol* begins with a capital letter "C" because it is the name of the building. In this case, the letter "c" makes the /k/ sound. Ask students what sound they hear at the end of the word. Practice making the /l/ sound. Ask students if they recognize any words in the sentence. While pointing to the words, read the sentences. Then have students read with you. Read the sentences again, and have students clap their hands when they hear the word *Capitol*.

Building Knowledge and Comprehension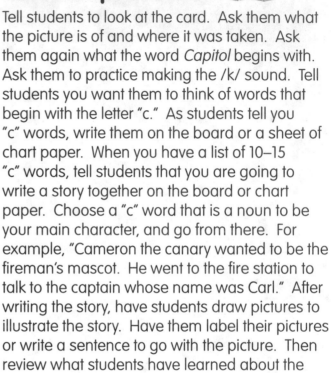

Tell students to look at the card. Ask them what the picture is of and where it was taken. Ask them again what the word *Capitol* begins with. Ask them to practice making the /k/ sound. Tell students you want them to think of words that begin with the letter "c." As students tell you "c" words, write them on the board or a sheet of chart paper. When you have a list of 10–15 "c" words, tell students that you are going to write a story together on the board or chart paper. Choose a "c" word that is a noun to be your main character, and go from there. For example, "Cameron the canary wanted to be the fireman's mascot. He went to the fire station to talk to the captain whose name was Carl." After writing the story, have students draw pictures to illustrate the story. Have them label their pictures or write a sentence to go with the picture. Then review what students have learned about the Capitol building.

Time to Differentiate!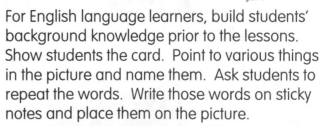

For English language learners, build students' background knowledge prior to the lessons. Show students the card. Point to various things in the picture and name them. Ask students to repeat the words. Write those words on sticky notes and place them on the picture.

For below-level students, preview the card in a small group. Read the words at the top of the card and ask students to repeat them. While pointing to each word, read the sentences at the bottom of the card. Repeat this several times.

Capitol

This is the United States **Capitol**.
It is in Washington, D.C.

PHOTO CREDIT: PHOTODISC

Activating Prior Knowledge

Ask students to look at the picture on Social Studies Card 26 and describe what they see. Ask them if they recognize the man in the picture. Ask students if they know the man's name. Talk with them about how most adults have jobs. Some people work outside of their home and others work at home. Explain to students that this man's name is George Washington and he was the first president of the United States of America. Ask them if they have an idea what jobs the president does. Tell them the president lives in Washington, D.C., and he works very hard to keep the United States safe and running smoothly. Read any books you may have about the president and the job he does.

Language Development

Ask students to look at the card again. Ask them to tell you who the person is and what he does for a job. Tell them to direct their attention to the word at the top of the card. Ask students if they can tell you what the word begins with. Ask them to practice making the /pr/ blend. Ask them if they recognize the sound at the end of the word. Have students practice making the /t/ sound. Point to the word *president* and read it to the class. Then point to the word while the class reads it. Ask students if they recognize any words in the sentence. While pointing to the words, read the sentence to students. Read the sentence and ask students to read it along with you. Tell students to think of an action they could show when they read the word *president*, for example, snapping their fingers or clapping. Read the sentence again and have students show the agreed-upon action.

Building Knowledge and Comprehension

Show students the card. Ask them who the man is in the picture. Ask them to tell you some important things he does. Talk to students about some of his jobs (e.g., keeping the United States safe, being the leader of American military forces, making sure American schools have good teachers). Tell them how he approves laws to help make the United States a better place. Discuss what students would do if they were president. After a short discussion, give students paper and ask them to write about or draw what they would do if they were president. Give them the prompt, "If I were president, I would _____." Have students draw a picture to go with their writing. Students should each share their pictures and writing with the rest of the class. Make a list of students' ideas and tally how many students had the same ideas.

Time to Differentiate!

For English language learners, scaffold the Building Knowledge and Comprehension lesson. After students have drawn their pictures of what they would do if they were president, label their pictures. Then encourage each student to use the label to complete his or her sentence.

For below-level students, practice identifying the beginning and ending sounds of the word *president*. If needed, tell students what each sound is and have them repeat the sound after you. Name other words that begin with the letter "p," and have students repeat the words, emphasizing the /p/ sound at the beginning.

PHOTO CREDIT: LUKE FRAZZA/AP

president

The **president** of the United States is the leader of the country. George Washington was the first president of the United States.

Activating Prior Knowledge

Show students Social Studies Card 27. Ask them to look at the card closely and describe what they see. Ask students what they think the girl might be thinking about. Allow time for students to share their thoughts. Talk to students about the word *pledge* and what it means. Ask students when in their life they would make a pledge. Talk about the students' responses as a class. For example, people sometimes make a pledge before they join a club, and sometimes a person makes a pledge or a promise to another person. When immigrants become citizens of the United States, they make a pledge. Ask students if they can think of a definition for the word *pledge*. Write the students' definition on the board. Look up the word *pledge* in the dictionary and write this definition on the board. Discuss the similarities and differences between the two.

Language Development

Show students the card. Ask them to look at the word at the top of the card. Ask them if any of them remember what the word is. Tell them that the word is *pledge* and ask them if they can remember what the definition of this word is. Explain that to make a pledge is to make a promise. Tell students that the word *pledge* begins with the letters "p" and "l" and have them practice making the /pl/ blend. On chart paper, list other /pl/ blend words that students suggest. Use each word in a sentence. Direct students' attention to the sentence at the bottom of the card. Ask them if they recognize any words in the sentence. While pointing to the words, read the sentence to students. Ask them to read the sentence with you while you point to the words.

Building Knowledge and Comprehension

Show students the card. Ask them to tell you what the word *pledge* means. Tell them that each school has a pledge to the community it exists within or a mission statement that they believe. Invite the school principal to come to the classroom and share with your class the school's pledge or mission statement. Ask the principal to explain it to the students using words that they will understand. After students understand that the school makes a promise to the community, ask students what they could promise to do for the school. For example, the students could promise or pledge to always do their best and be honest. Record students' ideas on the board or a sheet of chart paper. Have students each draw a picture of something they can do for the school. Give students the writing prompt, "I pledge to _____." Make the students' pages into a class book. Invite the principal back to class to read the book. Display the book in the school library or in the office for other students to see.

Time to Differentiate!

For English language learners, scaffold the writing activity in the Building Knowledge and Comprehension lesson. Ask students to share their ideas for pledges. Say each sentence you compose and have students repeat it before writing it on a large sheet of paper.

For below-level students, scaffold the writing activity in the Building Knowledge and Comprehension lesson. Encourage students to say their sentences out loud before writing them down.

pledge

A **pledge** is a promise we make.

Activating Prior Knowledge

Show students Social Studies Card 28. Ask them to describe what they see in the picture. Point out that there are many words and that there is a flag in the background. Ask them why there is a flag and what it represents. Tell them that the words are the Pledge of Alligiance, or a promise that Americans make to the flag. Read the Pledge of Allegiance to students, pointing to each word as you read. Then read the card again, asking students to join in. Ask students to share what the Pledge of Allegiance means to them. Write students' responses on the board or on chart paper. Write each line of the Pledge of Allegiance on a sentence strip. Mix up the order of the sentence strips and ask students to put the Pledge of Allegiance back in the right order. Practice reading the Pledge of Allegiance several times.

Language Development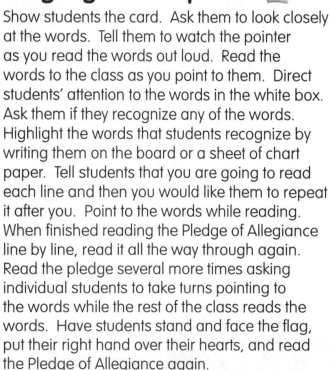

Show students the card. Ask them to look closely at the words. Tell them to watch the pointer as you read the words out loud. Read the words to the class as you point to them. Direct students' attention to the words in the white box. Ask them if they recognize any of the words. Highlight the words that students recognize by writing them on the board or a sheet of chart paper. Tell students that you are going to read each line and then you would like them to repeat it after you. Point to the words while reading. When finished reading the Pledge of Allegiance line by line, read it all the way through again. Read the pledge several more times asking individual students to take turns pointing to the words while the rest of the class reads the words. Have students stand and face the flag, put their right hand over their hearts, and read the Pledge of Allegiance again.

Building Knowledge and Comprehension

Show students the card. Ask them to read the card with you while you point to the words. Tell students to watch the pointer very closely and to read each word only when it is pointed to. As you point to the words, stop the pointer occasionally to make sure the students are watching the pointer. This activity will help students develop voice-print correspondence. Talk with students about what a pledge is and tell them that they are going to write a class pledge. Ask them to think of what they could pledge, as a class, to help them have a successful year. Record their ideas on the board or a sheet of chart paper. Take a class vote and agree upon the top ideas. Write a final pledge on a sheet of chart paper and display it in the classroom. Ask students to copy it on a sheet of paper and draw a picture to go along with the words. Read the class pledge many times throughout the school year.

Time to Differentiate!

For English language learners, help them learn the Pledge of Allegiance if they do not already know it. Say each line and then ask students to repeat it. Practice this several times.

For below-level students, help them see the connection between the words, which they may already have memorized, and the words on the card. Point to each word as you say it. Then have various students point to the words as you read the Pledge of Allegiance as a group.

Pledge of Allegiance

I Pledge Allegiance
to the flag of the
United States of America
and to the Republic
for which it stands,
one Nation under God,
indivisible, with liberty
and justice for all.

Unit 4
The United States

Introductory Lesson—Part A

Objective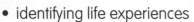

Pre-K and K–2 Standard 6.5: Students relate stories to their own lives and personal experiences.

Skills

- identifying life experiences
- connecting life experiences to text events
- locating information in text

Materials

- chalk or whiteboard markers
- chalkboard or whiteboard
- Social Studies Cards 24–28
- newspaper article from local newspaper, written about a child close in age to your students

Word Study

- United States
- America
- flag
- Capitol
- president
- leader
- experiences
- similarities
- differences
- pledge
- allegiance
- republic
- nation
- indivisible
- liberty
- justice

Comprehension and Skills

Part 1: Lesson Length: approx. 15 minutes

1. Hold up Social Studies Cards 24–28. As you hold up each card, have students raise their hands and tell you what each card reminds them of in their lives. Explain that everything we read can remind us of things in our lives. It is important to recognize these connections in order to understand what we are reading.

2. Now hold up Social Studies Card 24. Read the card to students and encourage them to follow along. Point to the word *flag* and read it. Point to the word *stars* and read it. Continue in this manner with the word *stripes*. Then read the sentence at the bottom. Discuss the vocabulary words and ask students to share experiences that connect their lives to these words.

3. Display Social Studies Card 26. Read the card to students and encourage them to follow along. Read the sentences at the bottom of the card, pointing to each word. Ask students to share experiences that connect to *president* and *United States of America*.

Introductory Lesson—Part A *(cont.)*

Comprehension and Skills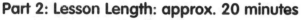

Part 2: Lesson Length: approx. 20 minutes

1. On the board, write things that students may have done over the summer. As you discuss what they did, write the names of students under corresponding categories.

2. Explain that we can read about people who have had similar experiences to ours. Explain that it is important to look for similarities in life experiences when we read to help us understand what we are reading.

3. Have students think about what they did yesterday. Encourage them to discuss their experiences with other students. Then ask, "What were the similarities? What were the differences?"

4. Locate a newspaper article that was written about a child close in age to your students. After reading the article, ask students to share if they have had similar experiences. Ask them to explain why it is important to recognize similar experiences in books and reading materials.

Comprehension and Skills

Part 3: Lesson Length: approx. 20 minutes

1. Tell students that they are going to be reading detectives, so they need to be able to ask good questions. Explain that asking good questions can help us understand what we are reading. On the board, write the following words: *allegiance, republic, nation, indivisible, liberty,* and *justice.* Read the words to students and tell them you will be discussing them soon.

2. Hold up Social Studies Card 27. Read the word *pledge* together. Now hold up Social Studies Card 28 and read the word *Pledge* again. As a class, read the remaining words *of Allegiance.* Read aloud the Pledge of Allegiance, pointing to each word as you read. Then chorally read the pledge.

3. Focus on each word of the pledge. Have students ask questions to help figure out the meaning of each word. Explain that good questions ask specific things about the word. Discuss the meanings of the words and how asking questions helped students get to the answers. Some of these words are difficult for students to understand. Use these definitions to help:

   - allegiance—a promise to stay together
   - republic—a place where lots of people help run the country
   - nation—country
   - indivisible—you can't break it up
   - liberty—free, freedom
   - justice—fair

Assessment

Hold up Social Studies Cards 24–28 for each student. Ask each student to explain how these cards are reminders of experiences in his or her life. Reiterate the importance of making connections when reading.

Unit 4
The United States

Focus Lesson

Objective

Pre-K and K–2 Standard 6.5: Students relate stories to their own lives and personal experiences.

Skills

- identifying life experiences
- connecting life experiences to text events
- locating information in text

Materials

- Social Studies Cards 24 and 26
- copies of Activity 26 for students (page 168)
- American flag

Word Study

- flag
- United States
- America
- president
- leader

Comprehension and Skills

Part 1: Lesson Length: approx. 20 minutes

1. Tell students that you are thinking of something in the classroom and you want them to guess what it is. Clues might include statements such as, "It is made of cloth. It has red on it. We see it every day. It has blue on it. It is very important to us. It has white on it. It has stars on it." Continue giving clues until someone guesses the flag.

2. Hold up Social Studies Card 24 for students to see. Ask them to tell you what this card is about, using questions such as, "Do the pictures help us? Do the words help us? Have we ever seen anything that is on this card?" Explain that recognizing things that are familiar helps us understand more of what we read. Students should recognize the flag on the card.

3. Using the card, instruct students to sound out the words on the card. Begin with the letter "f." Ask, "What sound does 'f' make?" Continue in this manner, making the sound of each letter of the word *flag*. Help students sound out the word.

4. Read the sentence at the bottom of the card to students. Point to each word in the sentence as you read. Discuss the meaning of the words *United States* and *America*.

5. Instruct students to be on the lookout for flags. They are to locate as many American flags in as many places as possible. Have them report to the class on the number of flags they located. Ask students to describe what the American flag looks like and where we might see the American flag on display.

Focus Lesson (cont.)

Comprehension and Skills

Part 2: Lesson Length: approx. 20 minutes

1. Hold up Social Studies Card 26 and ask students to read the words on the card. Read the word *president* together while reviewing the sounds each letter makes. Then point to each word as you read the sentences at the bottom of the page. Read the sentences with students. Ask students to identify the person in the picture.

2. Have students imagine that the president of the United States is visiting your classroom. Ask them what they would ask or say to the president. Allow students time to share their questions or comments with the class. Distribute copies of Activity 26 (page 168). Explain that you would like them to write what they would say to the president. You may choose to have students do this activity at their seats or you can place the pages at a center and invite small groups to do the activity. You may want to do this activity when you are available to help with spelling and word choice, as this activity may be difficult for students to do independently.

3. Encourage students to share their pages with the rest of the class. Did students have similar questions and comments? Ask students, "What do you think the president would say if he were really visiting the classroom? What clarification questions would you want to ask?" Discuss students' ideas as a class. Discuss the difference between large, thinking questions and small, clarifying questions.

Time to Differentiate!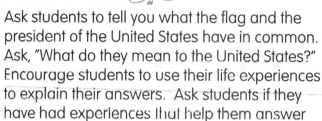

For above-level students, have them classify their questions as either large, thinking questions or small, clarifying questions. Challenge them to justify their groupings.

Assessment

Ask students to tell you what the flag and the president of the United States have in common. Ask, "What do they mean to the United States?" Encourage students to use their life experiences to explain their answers. Ask students if they have had experiences that help them answer these questions.

Center Activities

Objective

Pre-K and K–2 Standard 6.5: Students relate stories to their own lives and personal experiences.

Center #1:
Where's the Flag?

Materials

- Social Studies Card 24
- student copies of Activity 24 (page 166)
- crayons, colored pencils, or markers
- American flag

Comprehension and Skills

1. Hold up Social Studies Card 24 and ask students to read the words on the card. Begin by sounding out the word *flag* and then have students read the sentence at the bottom of the card. Review the meaning of the words *United States of America*.

2. Ask students if they have ever seen a flag before. Ask them to share the places where they have seen the American flag. Ask, "How is the flag of the United States different from the state flag?" Ask students to locate the flag in your classroom. Ask them, "Is the flag in the classroom the same as the flag on this card?"

3. Ask students, "What colors are on the flag? What do these colors represent?" Discuss the flag and the meaning of the colors and symbols of the American flag. (The stars represent the 50 states in the United States. The stripes represent the 13 original colonies. The blue stands for freedom and justice. The red represents the blood of those who have fought for our freedom. The white represents the purity of the nation.)

4. Distribute student copies of Activity 24 (page 166) to students at a center. Have students look at the page while you explain that they are to draw pictures of places where they have seen the American flag. Have them include a picture of the flag. Place this card in a prominent place so that students may refer to it as they make their drawings. Students may use crayons, colored pencils, or markers.

5. Have students share the pictures they have drawn with the class, explaining what the colors and symbols on the flag represent. Ask students to tell you what these symbols and colors remind them of.

Center Activities *(cont.)*

Center #2:
I Pledge Allegiance

Materials

- Social Studies Card 27
- student copies of Activity 27 (page 169)
- crayons, colored pencils, or markers

Comprehension and Skills

1. Hold up Social Studies Card 27 and ask students to read the words on the card. Read the word *pledge* together while reviewing the sounds of each letter. Read the sentence at the bottom of the card and point to each word as you read it. Read the sentence again and encourage students to read along with you. Have them review with you what the girl is doing. Ask, "What do we need to remember when we say the pledge?" Have students demonstrate how to stand when saying the pledge. Ask them to close their eyes and picture themselves saying the Pledge of Allegiance.

2. Brainstorm with students a list of places where people say the Pledge of Allegiance. (Your list may include in school, at special programs, at sporting events, or on Independence Day.) Ask students to think about why the pledge is said at these places and times. Encourage students to draw upon personal experience to answer the question.

3. Distribute copies of Activity 27 (page 169) at the center. Have students look at the page while you explain that you would like each of them to draw a picture of themselves saying the Pledge of Allegiance. Students may use crayons, colored pencils, or markers.

4. Encourage students to share their pictures with the rest of the class. Point out the similarities that these drawings share, noting that they have had similar experiences in saying the pledge. Instruct students to use their pictures as a guide to share what they have learned about the Pledge of Allegiance.

5. Set up a rotation in your class to allow one student per day to lead the class in the Pledge of Allegiance. Determine the location where the student will stand and what this student's role will be. You may choose to model the expected student behaviors. Discuss what this student needs to remember about the pledge. How can the other students in the class show respect for the flag by saying the Pledge of Allegiance? As time goes on, discuss the experiences that students have while leading the pledge.

Unit 4
The United States

Introductory Lesson—Part B

Objectives

Pre-K Standard 5.11: Students use emergent reading skills to "read" a story (e.g., gather meaning from words and pictures).

K–2 Standard 7.1: Students use reading skills and strategies to understand a variety of informational texts.

Skills

- recognizing larger, thought-provoking questions
- recognizing smaller, clarification questions
- determining the difference between larger and smaller questions about text

Materials

- Social Studies Cards 24–28

Word Study

- Capitol
- United States
- Washington, D.C.
- America
- flag
- pledge
- allegiance
- president
- leader
- republic
- nation
- indivisible
- liberty
- justice
- experiences
- similarities

Comprehension and Skills

Part 1: Lesson Length: approx. 15 minutes

1. Students are to listen carefully as you read two different sentences.

   Sentence #1: What is your name?

   Sentence #2: My name is John.

   Ask, "How are these two sentences different?" Allow time for discussion, then explain that one of the sentences is a question. Demonstrate how the voice rises when a question is being asked. Certain types of questions help us understand what we are reading.

2. Hold up Social Studies Card 25. Ask students to help you figure out what this card is about. Have them think of and share questions they could ask to understand more about it.

3. Ask students to listen to the following questions and put their thumbs up if they think it is a good question. If it is not a very helpful question, have them put their thumbs down.

   - Where is the Capitol? (thumbs up)
   - Why is the grass green in this picture? (thumbs down)
   - What do people do at the Capitol? (thumbs up)
   - Why are there trees by the Capitol? (thumbs down)

Introductory Lesson—Part B *(cont.)*

Comprehension and Skills

Part 2: Lesson Length: approx. 15 minutes

1. Hold up Social Studies Card 27. Ask students to help you figure out what this card is about. Have them share questions they could ask to understand more about it.

2. Ask students to listen to the following questions and put their thumbs up if they think it is a good question. If it is not a very helpful question, have them put their thumbs down.

   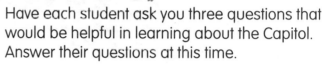

   - What does the word *pledge* mean? (thumbs up)
   - What did this girl eat for breakfast? (thumbs down)
   - Why does she have her hand over her heart? (thumbs up)
   - How old is the girl in the picture? (thumbs down)

3. Repeat this process of asking questions for the Social Studies Cards 24, 26, and 28.

4. Explain the difference between large, thinking questions and small, clarifying questions. Point out that small, clarifying questions help us to understand what we read.

Assessment

Have each student ask you three questions that would be helpful in learning about the Capitol. Answer their questions at this time.

Unit 4
The United States

Focus Lesson

Objectives

Pre-K Standard 5.11: Students use emergent reading skills to "read" a story (e.g., gather meaning from words and pictures).

K–2 Standard 7.1: Students use reading skills and strategies to understand a variety of informational texts.

Skills

- recognizing larger, thought-provoking questions
- recognizing smaller, clarification questions
- determining the difference between larger and smaller questions about text

Materials

- Social Studies Cards 25 and 28
- white paper and crayons
- chalkboard or whiteboard
- chalk or whiteboard markers

Word Study

- Capitol
- United States
- Washington, D.C.
- Pledge of Allegiance
- United States of America
- promise

Comprehension and Skills

Part 1: Lesson Length: approx. 20 minutes

1. Gather students in a circle and ask the following questions: "What do you do when you go to the dentist? The grocery store? The zoo? The post office? Your school? The movies?" Explain that there are many different types of buildings where we live and we go to these buildings for different reasons. Ask, "Wouldn't it be silly if we went to the school to buy our groceries? Or if we went to the zoo to watch a movie?"

2. Explain that you have a picture of a building that you would like to show them. Say to students, "This is a building that is not in our city (or town), but it is very important to us." Show students the picture of the Capitol building on Social Studies Card 25. Tell them that this is the Capitol building. Read the word *Capitol* with students by sounding out each letter. Then read the sentences at the bottom with students as you point to each word. Discuss the meaning of the words *United States*, *Capitol*, and *Washington, D.C.*

3. Now that you have read the card, explain what happens in the Capitol building. People work in the Capitol building to make the laws for the United States.

Focus Lesson *(cont.)*

Comprehension and Skills

Part 2: Lesson Length: approx. 20 minutes

1. As a class, make a list of the things that you do together at the beginning of each school day. List responses on the board. Students will probably suggest that the class recites the Pledge of Allegiance. Discuss why we say the Pledge of Allegiance every day.

2. Ask students to show you what they do during the pledge. As a class, recite the Pledge of Allegiance.

3. Pair up students. One student acts as a statue. The other student moves the arms, legs, head, and hands of the statue to the correct position for saying the Pledge of Allegiance. Then have students switch roles.

4. Together discuss why we stand a certain way and say certain things during the pledge. Ask for volunteers to demonstrate how we should not stand when we say the pledge.

5. Give students blank paper and crayons, and have them draw a picture of what they are thinking as they say the Pledge of Allegiance. If time allows, share the pictures with the class. You can bind the pictures together to create a class book.

Comprehension and Skills

Part 3: Lesson Length: approx. 20 minutes

1. Hold up Social Studies Card 28 and read it with students. Call on students to come up and locate these words: *pledge*, *allegiance*, *United States*, *America*, *republic*, *stands*, *nation*, *God*, *indivisible*, *liberty*, and *justice*. Emphasize the sounds of each word to help them locate the words on the card.

2. Allow time for students to ask questions about the Pledge of Allegiance, but do not answer them at this point. Write each question on the board, categorizing them into two categories: "Large, Thinking Questions" and "Small, Clarifying Questions." Then read each question again and answer it. Discuss the differences between the two types of questions. Explain how the small, clarifying questions can help us make sense of what we are reading. These questions can also help us understand new words.

3. Ask students to tell you what they are reminded of by the words in the pledge. What do they think of when they hear these words?

Time to Differentiate!

For above-level students, have students create posters that represent one of the words taught in this unit. Allow time for students to share and describe their posters to the class.

Assessment

Have students draw a picture of the Capitol building showing the people inside. Each student should also explain the activities that occur inside the building.

Center Activities

Objectives

Pre-K Standard 5.11: Students use emergent reading skills to "read" a story (e.g., gather meanings from words and pictures).

K–2 Standard 7.1: Students use reading skills and strategies to understand a variety of informational texts.

Center #1: The Capitol Building

Materials

- Social Studies Card 25
- student copies of Activity 25 (page 167)
- crayons, colored pencils, or markers

Comprehension and Skills

1. Hold up Social Studies Card 25 and ask students to read the words on the card. Begin by sounding out the word *Capitol* and then have students read the sentences at the bottom of the card. Review the meaning of the words *United States*, *Capitol*, and *Washington, D.C.*

2. Review with students what the Capitol building is. Encourage them to ask clarification questions to help them understand what the Capitol is. Remind them to use the 5 Ws and H questions (who, what, where, why, when, and how). Use the following questions as a guide:
   - Where is the Capitol building?
   - How big is the Capitol?
   - Who works in the Capitol?
   - When do people go to the Capitol?
   - Why do people go to the Capitol?
   - What do people do at the Capitol?

3. Distribute copies of Activity 25 (page 167) to students at a center. Have students look at the page. Explain that you would like them to locate the people that they would expect to find at the Capitol. When they find these people, have them circle them and then color all the pictures on the page. Place Social Studies Card 25 in a prominent place at the center so that students may refer to it as they complete this activity. Students may use crayons, colored pencils, or markers.

Center Activities *(cont.)*

Center #2:
Pledge Questions

Materials

- Social Studies Card 28
- student copies of Activity 28 (page 170)
- crayons, colored pencils, or markers

Comprehension and Skills

1. Hold up Social Studies Card 28 and ask students to read the words on the card. Read the word *Pledge* together while reviewing the sounds of each letter. Then read the remaining words *of Allegiance* together. Next read the Pledge of Allegiance and point to each word as you read. Read the pledge again and encourage students to read along with you. Have students review with you the meaning of each of the words in the pledge. Help students come up with synonyms to replace the unknown words. Ask them to share any questions they may have about the Pledge of Allegiance.

2. Have students close their eyes and picture themselves saying the Pledge of Allegiance. Distribute copies of Activity 28 (page 170) to students at a center. Have students read and answer the questions on the page. Then have students color the page using crayons, colored pencils, or markers.

3. If time allows, have students stand one at a time and say the Pledge of Allegiance. See if students can say it without looking at the words. Discuss the following questions:
   - Why do we say the pledge every day?
   - Why does it matter how we stand during the pledge?
   - What do you think about the Pledge of Allegiance?
   - What do you think about when you say the Pledge of Allegiance?
   - What does the Pledge of Allegiance mean?
   - Where can you learn more about the Pledge of Allegiance?

Unit 4
The United States

Wrap-up

Introduction

The wrap-up activities tie together the skills that have been taught throughout the unit. They provide opportunities for students to show the skills they have learned within this unit.

Objectives

Pre-K and K–2 Standard 6.5: Students relate stories to their own lives and personal experiences.

Pre-K Standard 5.11: Students use emergent reading skills to "read" a story (e.g., gather meanings from words and pictures).

K–2 Standard 7.1: Students use reading skills and strategies to understand a variety of informational texts.

Materials

- Social Studies Cards 24–28
- crayons, markers, or colored pencils
- large sheets of chart paper
- student copies of page 165

Comprehension and Skills

1. Set aside a day to celebrate Patriotic Day, which would come at the end of the theme "The United States". On the specified day, instruct your students to wear the colors red, white, and blue. Again discuss the meaning of the colors on the flag of the United States.

2. Place one of Social Studies Cards 24–28 along with a large sheet of chart paper on different desks or tables in the classroom. Have students use crayons, markers, or colored pencils to draw pictures or write words that pertain to each card. Students should record what these cards remind them of from their lives. When all students have had a chance to record their ideas and experiences, discuss these ideas as a class.

3. Now post two large sheets of chart paper on the board. On one page, write "Big Questions." On the other page, write "Smaller Questions." Now is the time for students to share the questions that they still have about the country, the flag, the pledge, the president, or the Capitol of the United States. As they share their questions, record them on the chart paper. Ask students for input regarding whether their questions are large, thinking questions or small, clarifying questions. Then ask them to predict where they can go to get answers to their questions. If time allows, look for the answers to these questions.

4. Have students complete the activity on page 165.

The United States

Finish the sentences about the United States.

I am _____ .

My country _____ .

The flag _____ .

I hope _____ .

I like _____ .

I think the president should _____ .

The Pledge of Allegiance _____ .

I cannot _____ .

Questions that I have about the United States:

Why does the president _____ ?

When did the flag _____ ?

I wonder _____ .

Where is the _____ ?

What does _____ in the pledge mean?

Create some questions of your own:

_____ ?

_____ ?

_____ ?

Draw and label a place where you see the American **flag**. Draw the flag, too.

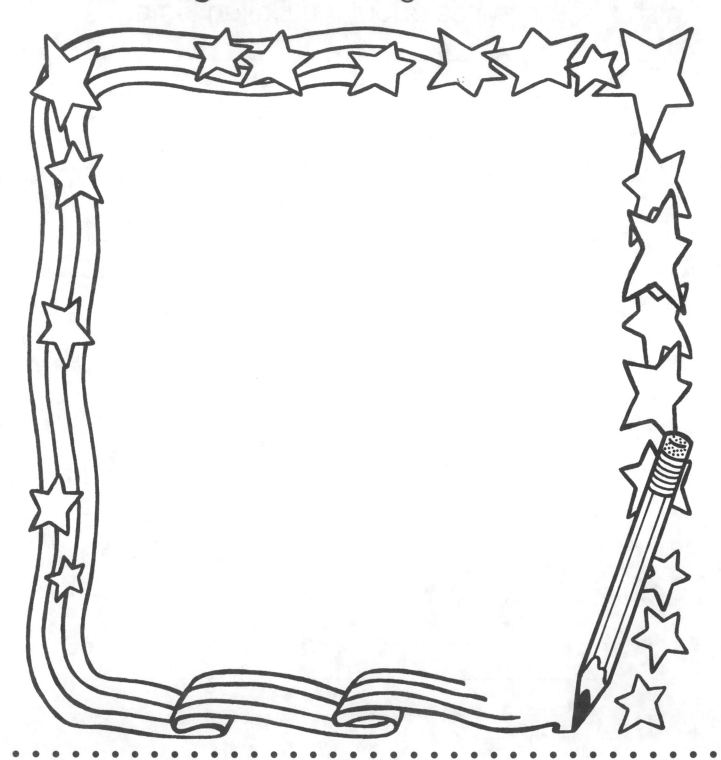

The **Capitol** is the building where people work to make laws. Circle the people you would expect to see working at the Capitol. Color the pictures.

Imagine you had a chance to meet the **president**. What would you say to him? Write your words below.

_____

- -

_____

_____

- -

_____

_____

- -

_____

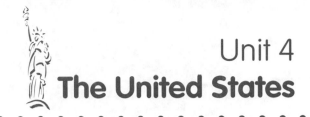
Think about a place where you say the Pledge of Allegiance. Draw yourself saying the **pledge** in that place.

Do you know the **Pledge of Allegiance**? Can you say it without looking at the words?

Teach the Pledge of Allegiance to someone who doesn't know it. It could be a younger brother or sister or a neighbor or friend. Say the Pledge of Allegiance together.

References Cited

Berry, R. 2001. Children's environmental print: Reliability, validity, and relationship to early reading. Doctoral dissertation, University of North Carolina at Chapel Hill.

Christie, J. F., B. J. Enz, M. Gerard, and J. Prior. 2002. Using environmental print as teaching materials and assessment tools. Paper presented at the International Reading Association annual convention, San Francisco, CA.

Christie, J. F., B. J. Enz, and C. Vukelich. 2002. *Teaching language and literacy, preschool through the elementary grades.* 2nd. ed. New York: Longman.

Csikszentmihalyi, M. 1990. *Flow: The psychology of optimal experience.* New York: Harper & Row Publishers.

Duke, N. K., and V. Purcell-Gates. 2003. Genres at home and at school: Bridging the known to the new. *The Reading Teacher* 57 (1): 30–37.

Ferreiro, E., and A. Teberosky. 1982. *Literacy before schooling.* Exeter, NH: Heinemann.

Goodman, Y. 1986. Children coming to know literacy. In *Emergent literacy: Writing and reading,* ed., W. H. Teale and E. Sulzby, 1–14. Norwood, NJ: Ablex.

Harste, J., C. Burke, and V. Woodward. 1982. Children's language and world: Initial encounters with print. In *Reader meets author/bridging the gap: A psycholinguistic and sociolinguistic perspective,* ed. J. A. Langer and M. T. Smith-Burke, 105–31. Newark, DE: International Reading Association.

NAEYC. 2001. What does it look like and what does it take?: Supporting early literacy. White House Summit on Early Childhood Cognitive Development, Washington, D.C.

National Institute of Child Health and Human Development. 2000. *Teaching children to read: An evidence-based assessment of the scientific research literature on reading and its implications for reading instruction.* Report of the National Reading Panel. Washington, D.C.: U.S. Government Print Office.

Orellana, M. F., and A. Hernandez. 2003. Talking the walk: Children reading urban environmental print. In *Promising practices for urban reading instruction,* ed., P. A. Mason and J. S. Schumm, 25–36. Newark, DE: International Reading Association.

Piaget, J. 1978. *Success and understanding.* Cambridge, MA: Harvard University Press.

Simmons, D., B. Gunn, S. Smith, and E. J. Kame'enui. 1994. Phonological awareness: Application of instructional design. LD Forum 19 (2): 7–10.

Tomlinson, C. 2000. *Leadership for Differentiating Schools and Classrooms.* Alexandria, VA: Association for Supervision and Curriculum Development.

U.S. Department of Education. 2000. *No Child Left Behind.* http://www.ed.gov/nclb/landing.html

U.S. Department of Education. 2001. *Early Reading First.* http://www.ed.gov/programs/earlyreading/index.html

Xu, S. H., and A. L. Rutledge. 2003. Chicken starts with ch! Kindergartners learn through environmental print. *Young Children* 58 (2): 44–51.

Notes

Notes

Notes

- -

- -

Notes